BUDDHA

and the

MAN

on the

CROSS

second edition

Norman Law

ISBN 979-8-88751-814-5 (paperback)
ISBN 979-8-88751-815-2 (digital)

Christian Faith Publishing
832 Park Avenue
Meadville, PA 16335
www.christianfaithpublishing.com

Printed in the United States of America

TRUE ENLIGHTENMENT:

The Prophecy:
Isaiah 9:2: "The people that walked in darkness have seen a GREAT LIGHT: they that dwell in the land of the shadow of death, upon them hath the light shined."

The Preparation for the coming of the LIGHT:
John 1:6–9: "There came a man sent from God, whose name was John. He came as a witness, to testify about the Light, so that all might believe through him. He was not the Light, but he came to testify about the Light. There was the true Light which, coming into the world, enlightens every man."

The Fulfilment of the Prophecy:
John 8:12: "Then Jesus again spoke to them, saying, 'I am the Light of the world; he who follows Me will not walk in the darkness, but will have the Light of life.'"

The Promise:
John 12:46: "Jesus said: 'I have come as Light into the world, so that everyone who believes in Me will not remain in darkness.'"

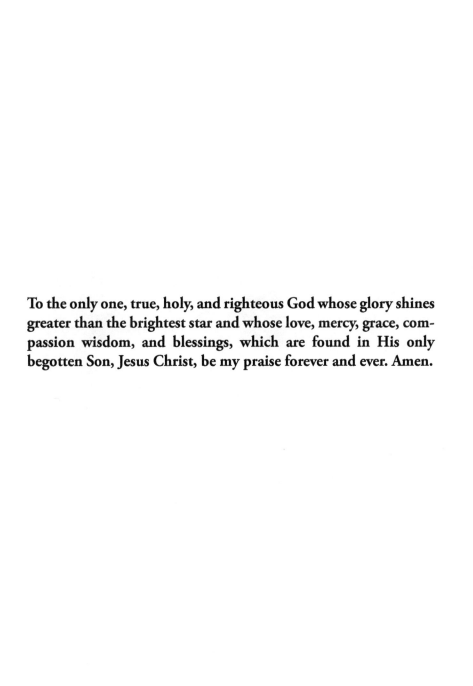

To the only one, true, holy, and righteous God whose glory shines greater than the brightest star and whose love, mercy, grace, compassion wisdom, and blessings, which are found in His only begotten Son, Jesus Christ, be my praise forever and ever. Amen.

Contents

This is written for the many people who are interested in the differences between the Buddhist and the Christian faiths, as well as knowing the basic doctrines and practices of both faiths. Faith that is not examined is not worth all the external showings or displays of piety or devotion, as it is like believing that *pigs can fly* because their parents or relatives told them so. Many Buddhists and Christians have inherited their so-called faiths from their parents, and even several generations before, and therefore do not really know what their faiths and practices entail. Many so-called Buddhists and Christians refuse to openly discuss what they believe because they feel uncomfortable, and this is probably due to the fact that they do not know the foundation or doctrine of their faith or the basis of their beliefs.

Many Asian parents still carry on the old Confucian thought that their children are there to obey and do that which they are told, and to not question what they are asked to do. The old Confucian teaching of respect for the parents and elders had been mistaken for complete obedience, which is a fallacy. Respect and obedience are two different ideas. Respect of a position because of the wisdom learned from experience and by virtue of being a parent, grandparent, or an elder is understandable. But to expect complete obedience from a younger person because of your age is foolhardy, as in this present age, the younger person will probably have greater knowledge assisted by the Internet than the older. It is true that younger children need obedience to their parents in certain aspects of life, but after reaching adulthood, there should no longer be that expectation of complete obedience. To honour and respect parents and elders is an interactive behaviour, such as the way we address and treat them, and that is very different than obedience. To honour and respect parents and elders is a good thing, but to blindly obey and sometimes disregard what is truthful is to betray oneself, as well as others in accepting and telling a lie. And in doing that, one sells his or her personal integrity and self-worth in order to please parents or elders.

It is ideal that young people be gradually taught independence of thought and decision-making all through their growing up years and not just handed to them on a platter upon adulthood. Under such tutelage of demanding respect, honour, and blind obedience, children are afraid to ask parents those questions that needed to be asked. Otherwise, they practiced their faith in ignorance. On one hand, they ask and challenge their children to be inquisitive, creative, and to learn and get an education in school. But on the other hand, they themselves do not practice what they preach. In a sense, they are just hypocrites, and their children see right through them. Obedience that is done blindly is not honor but a total lack of self-respect, and that is dishonourable. Generally speaking, you can especially see that in the workplace, a majority of employees from Asia are the most compliable and do not ask many questions, and therefore their contributions are as expected and seldom over and above the calling. They just do as they are told.

This writing is to open up the world for all to explore the tenets of their faith and the different aspects of Buddhism compared to that of Christianity. This is an introduction to the different beliefs of Buddhism and Christianity and is open and welcome to those who elect to delve deeper into the different faiths. There are so many sects in Buddhism, and it is impossible to cover everything in detail, so this writing condenses the main thoughts and basic doctrines of the Buddhist, as well as that of the Christian faiths. Buddhism is not static, as any Buddhist monk or nun, who felt if he or she had achieved a certain level and if they garnered a healthy respect from peers and in their sphere of influence, can write about their *new revelations* on how to achieve Nirvana or be a Bodhisattva. As a result, many schools of Buddhism had been established, each showing the hundreds of steps required to each level of monkhood in the quest for Nirvana or to be a Bodhisattva (for definition, please go to page 23). There is no one or very few to contest or have the sole authority to challenge or dispute any new revelations, and if so, he or she will just create another sect or school of Buddhism. It is no different in some ways of what is happening in Christianity today. Many so-called Christian groups started practicing many things that are contrary to or outside what are in the Bible and, therefore, do not in many ways resemble the early church. Most Buddhist groups will not attest or challenge any new thoughts or practices but will seek the middle way so as not to offend. The different Buddhist groups will dispute with the new thought or doctrine but will eventually back off. Essentially, Mahayana Buddhism practices the middle way.

Hopefully, this writing will assist in clearing up the perception of what are the beliefs and practices of Buddhism and Christianity. The person should also be able to take a clear stand of what his or her belief is and have a sound basis for his or her faith. One cannot continue to practice a faith or religion without truly consciously knowing the why and wherefore of the doctrines, rites, and beliefs. The pursuit of a faith or religion is akin to the search for truth. And that is a noble quest. And to pursue one and not explore others is to put blinders on the minds and thoughts and deny that there are other alternative answers to the same questions that plague mankind. The pursuit requires a certain amount of courage in that one should be able to look it straight in the eye and say, "I have been erroneous, and it is time to find one that is true." It is definitely not for the weak and feebleminded. We are living in an age of reason and knowledge, and we cannot any longer live in the shadow of superstitions, ignorance, fear, or hearsays. There is tremendous respect for anyone of any faith or religion that he or she elects to follow or believe, and all exploration of faiths is asking is that you should know what you have elected to believe and understand the basis of your faith and religion and substance to your beliefs and that we do not blindly accept what others purport to be true. Nevertheless, the respect still remains for the rights of anyone who elects to believe that pigs can fly.

In this second edition, the author will provide the sources of where Gautama Buddha got his doctrine of Enlightenment, Meditation and the Samsara cycle, which constitute the core Buddhist doctrines. The asterisk beside the word tells you that theology, doctrines, or teachings are derived from ancient Vedic Hindu sacred texts, and they can be found in the last chapter of the book under "Ancient Sacred Vedic Hindu Text References."

A. The Man: Gautama Siddhartha

Buddha is actually a title given to the man, Gautama Siddhartha, born around 563 BCE in Lumbini, according to Buddhist tradition, in the region of Nepal or Northeast India, and raised in the Shakya, capital of Kapilvastu. It is generally accepted that he passed away around 483 BCE. During his search for an answer to the suffering of this life, he was exposed to multiple Hindu schools of thought and meditative techniques that flourished during that time period in India. *Buddha* is a title accorded to a person who had overcome all manner of human cravings, lusts, greed, wants, and needs. From the Ancient Sacred Vedic Hindu Texts, it is obvious that Gautama Siddhartha was a very smart thinking person, who refined the popular beliefs and practices of the time to suit his own reasonings, and it is his followers that called it Buddhism, after Gautama Siddhartha.

B. Written Text (Buddhism)

General

No record of Gautama Siddhartha's own writings was found during his lifetime or a few centuries thereafter. One edict of Asoka the Great (269 BCE to 232 BCE) commemorates the king's pilgrimage to the Buddha's birthplace in Lumbini. Another one of his edicts mentions the titles of several Dharma texts, establishing the existence of a written Buddhist tradition at least by the time of the grandfather of King Asoka, King Chandragupta, founder of the Maurya empire between 322 BCE to 187 BCE. The word *Dhamma originated from Hindu Sanskrit, and in Buddhism, it means cosmic law and order, but it can also mean teachings of Buddha. These texts are possibly the precursor of the Buddhist's Pāli Canon, which is kept in Sri Lanka today.

The oldest surviving Buddhist manuscripts are supposedly found in eastern Afghanistan and now preserved in the British Library. They are written in the Gāndhārī language using the Kharosthi script on twenty-seven birch bark manuscripts and dated from the first century BC to the third century BC.

Gautama Buddha took and modified and refined the Vedic Hindu doctrines of *Enlightenment or *Self-realization, *Meditation, and the *Samsara cycle to suit his own thoughts and ideas and in some instances gave new terms for them. Gautama Buddha would have been exposed to the core Ancient Sacred Vedic Texts (Rig Veda, Samaveda, Yajur Veda, and the Atharvaveda) (1500–500 BC).

Hindu doctrines and teachings at the estimated time of when they were popular, as can be found in the major Upanishad (900–300 BCE), Bhagavad Gita (400–200 BCE), Mahabharata (400 BCE), and the Major Puranas (1000–250 BCE). The thoughts, ideas, and doctrines were around at the time of Vedic Hinduism even before it was put into writing and when the Gautama Buddha was around.

(i) The Tripitaka

The Pali Canon is the earliest and only collection of Buddhist scriptures in the Theravada Buddhist tradition preserved in the Pali language. It is suggested or thought to have been taught in Northern India, preserved orally until it was committed to writing during the Fourth Buddhist Council in Sri Lanka in 29 BC, and approximately 454 years after the death of Gautama Siddhartha. The Tripitaka is part of the Pali Canon. Tripitaka means the three baskets, and it is a collection of forty-five volumes and all in one modern edition.

The first basket is about rules and guidelines (about 227 regulations) for living a monastic life in a Sangha (monastery). The second basket contains Gautama Siddhartha's teachings and sermons on subjects like moral behaviour and is called the Discourse Basket (Sutra Pitaka). The third and final basket is a collection of miscellaneous short writings like poetry, songs, and stories of Gautama Siddhartha and his previous lives. None of these writings are by Gautama Siddhartha himself.

(ii) The Sutras

Followers of Mahayana Buddhism respect the Tripitaka as a holy text, but they add to it some over two thousand or so-called sacred texts to the writings, and most of them are under the heading of sutras. That happened around the second century BC when the split between the Theravada and Mahayana occurred. Any monk who believes that he had achieved Buddhahood can write his own sutra or sacred text, and as a result, there are many different sutras, like the Pure Land Sutras, the Lotus Sutras, the Heart Sutras, Land Bliss Sutras, etc. So each has its very own teachings with regards to different aspects of the path toward Nirvana.

(iii) Nagarjuna

Nagarjuna founded one of the Mahayana school and wrote the Sutra on the Middle Way (Madhyamika) and interpreted the Sutra of the Perfection of Wisdom, which elaborated the idea of Emptiness and Impermanence, in that everything is in an eternal state of change, and so does its inter-relativity among itself.

(iv) Vajrayana Buddhism

Vajrayana drew from the different Buddhist schools of thought but draws extensively from the Mahayana sutras, as well as Nagarjuna. Vajrayana Buddhists use tantric texts. Its tantric practices are copied from the wandering Hindu *Yogis in Northern India during the medieval period (~third to the tenth century), but not all the *Yogi rites are copied. As a result, Vajrayana Buddhism developed a large quantity of text called the Buddhist Tantras or the equivalent of the *Vedic Hindu Mantram. It has many types of tantras. The kriya tantras are used for healing illnesses, generating wealth, and even trying to control the weather. Then there is the Yoga Tantra, which focuses on the liberation of the self, as well as five other Buddhist tantras for an assortment of functions. There are many more different kinds of tantras that goes from one extreme to another, like using alcohols, sexual yoga, and practices that is said to evoke wrathful deities to astrology.

Comments

Gautama Siddhartha had never claimed to possess eternal omniscience or eternal transcendence, neither did the earlier Buddhist texts like the Agamas or Nikayas. However, living in a superstitious time and society, supernatural abilities were later accorded to the Buddha. It is only in the later Mahayana sutras and later Pali commentaries that such claims start to appear. The Agama is a collection of early Buddhist scriptures or works, and in Theravada Buddhism, it is called Nikayas.

Gautama Buddha took the doctrine of attaining the *Atman (Universal Spirit, union with Brahma, Krishna, or Vishnu thus achieving immortality and called it "Enlightenment." In Hinduism, the path to Buddhist "Enlightenment" is called *"Self-Realization," and it is through *meditation, *yogic or otherwise, for the total abandonment or *Renunciation of all desires, wants, needs, feelings, etc., and it the same with Buddhism. Some sects of Buddhism took the doctrine of continual rebirths through the *Samsara cycle but said that at each rebirth, it is "different person" because the soul is changing continually.

At this present day, the head monks from any of the different sects or schools who feel that they are *enlightened* can write or produce new revelations or tantric techniques on how to achieve Buddhahood or Nirvana. Therefore, the recommended path to *enlightenment* takes many routes depending on the sect or Buddhist schools that you listen to.

(v) Written Text (Christian Text)

The practice of Christianity is based on the sixty-six books, of which thirty-nine are classified as Old Testament written by twenty-four prophets, and twenty-seven are classified as New Testament written by ten authors, some of whom were apostles and church elders, all over the period from about 1400 BC to AD 90. The most amazing thing about the sixty-six books is that what were written testifies and complements each other in terms of information, instructions, doctrines, and prophesies. Prophesies in the Bible are regarded as inspired words of God that predict and foretell future events. There are some three thousand prophecies in the Bible, and over two thousand had been fulfilled, while the remaining are waiting to be fulfilled. There are no prophecies in any of the Buddhist texts or manuscripts. The Bible is regarded as the inspired *Word of God.* The first five books (Pentateuch) of the Bible can be found in the Jewish Torah. The Roman Catholics, the largest so-called *Christian sect or cult,* had adopted six more books in their Bible, therefore some of their practices are very different from *mainstream* (Protestants and Evangelicals) Christianity.

In this present world, it is impossible to find two books that testify and complement one another and without disagreeing concepts and teachings, much less to find sixty-six books by twenty-four different authors that testify and complement each other and written over a period of 3,400 years. It is really mind-boggling and truly deserving of your consideration and exploration. So the scriptures from the Bible are quoted in this discussion to support the doctrines and teachings of *mainstream* Christian beliefs. The manner in which scriptures are quoted is by identifying the name of the book of the Bible, and then the chapter and verses. To practice doctrines and beliefs outside what is written in the Bible is regarded as Christian heresy. An isolated scripture does not make a doctrine or constitute a belief.

One major concept in Christianity is that it must be based on the words in the scriptures as found in the Bible, and if it is outside that of the Bible, it is no longer considered as part of its doctrines, belief systems, and faith. Otherwise, anyone can introduce all kinds of outside teachings into the church belief systems and practices, like yoga, worshipping of idols or deities, chanting, or prayer beads, etc.

Comment: Not once in any of the Buddhist teachings can you find the Buddhist monks or promoters of Buddhism say that this part of the teaching comes from this or that part of the Pali Canon or the Dharma. Even with the (a) Eightfold Path and (b) Four Noble Truths, no one ever told or informed the listener as to where in the Pali Canon or Dharma can they be found. Similar doctrine in Hinduism can be found in the "Eight Paths of the *dharma found in the Mahabharata. Whereas in Christianity, a teaching, belief, and/ or practice must be found in the Bible with supporting scriptures. A single verse in the Bible does not make a doctrine. For more on the Hindu doctrine of dharma, please go to chapter 35.

2

Beginning of Buddhism
(Before 400 BC)

ANCIENT GODS

The thousands of gods of the ancient Mitanni (1500 BC to 1300 BC), Hittites (1600 BC–1180 BC), Hurrian, Kassites, Canaanites, and Sumerians had ceased to exist today in Turkey, Syria, Iraq, Israel, and Iran but continues to be worshipped in India and Southeast Asia. They just changed their names, but most of their roles and titles remained unchanged. It first moved into the Indus Valley civilization, then to the whole of India, where it is practiced today as Hinduism with its thousands of gods. Later, it is carried to Southeast Asia and morphed into Buddhism, but many of the deities remain the same, and the pantheon of gods and idols showed up with other names and looks or appearances. Not only do they share the same gods but also the Sanskrit language. Some form of the ancient Sanskrit language is found in the Hittites, Persian, Latin, Greek, German, and even the Northern Slavic languages.

There are many claims as to who really are the Indo-Aryan people that settled into the Indus Valley civilization and brought with them their language, gods, and idols. The Sumerian people have over three thousand gods, and the people of India have even more in their Hindu religion, and they even have similar ceremonies.

The major gods in the Hindu pantheons are Brahma, Vishnu, and Shiva, which represents the creator, sustainer, and destroyer are similar to the Persian gods of Tiamat, Enkil, and Marduk. The major Hindu and Persian gods have many avatars and reincarnations, and there are thousands of minor gods and demigods.

An early written inscription was discovered invoking Varuna as well as the gods Mitra (a vedic deity associated with the sky and later with waters, justice, and truth), Indra (a vedic god of the thunder and rain and is a great warrior, a symbol of courage and strength), and Nasatya (they are one of the two vedic twin doctor gods, sons of Saranyu, goddess of the cloud. Dasara and Nasatya are devas of the Ayurvedic medicine) was found in the treaty between Suppililiuma and Shattiwaza in the kingdom of Matanni, as large state in Northern Syria and Southeastern Anatolia around 1380 BC. The transcription from cuneiform reads a-ru-na, u-ru-wa-na equivalent the Vedic Varuna. These are the gods invoked by the Matanni kings, which supports the fact that the Mitanni people had accepted the Arya gods as theirs and later to become gods of the people in the Indus Valley Civilization. The Matanni empire was later conquered by the Hittites and thus the assimilation of gods and language. There are major similarities between the Sanskrit and the Avestan (Persian-Zoroastrain) language.

In East Asian Buddhism, Varuna (Hindu god) is one of the twelve deities (guardian of deities found in Buddhist temples). Varuna is called Shuitian in Chinese and Suiten (watery sky) in Japanese. Varuna joins the other eleven Hindu deities: Indra (Taishakeuten in Japanese); Agni (Katen), Yama (Emmaten), Nirrti (Rasetsuten); Vayu (Futen), Ishana (Ishanaten), Kubera (Tamonten); Brahma (Bonten); Prithvi (Chiten); Surya (Nitten), and Chandra (Gatten). Suiten was incorporated into Shinto Buddhism in Japan.

In the Mahayana Sutra, the Lotus Sutra mentioned Shiva as an emanation of Avalokiteshvara. In here, the Buddha described Avalokiteshvara as being able to take on numerous forms like Shravaka, Brahma, Yaksha, Gandharva including Shiva to teach the dharma to the people.

In Chinese Buddhism, the goddess Kuanyin had been a male divinity Avalokiteshvara Bodhisattva till the eighth century. Chinese Buddhism took root in China in AD 54 during the Han Dynasty (206 BC–AD 221). After the eighth century, the Indian influence has all but been erased, but the Chinese tradition gained prominence in image making, and in this case the Buddhist chief divinity, namely Avalokiteshvara Bodhisattva was worshipped and recognized in Indian form up to the beginning of the Sung Dynasty (AD 960–1279). After that, the male Avalokiteshvara has been represented as a female goddess of mercy. A necklace on her long neck, a rosary, a roll of prayers, and pearl are emblems given to her in her many portrayals on the Ming (AD 1368–1644) and Ching (AD 1644–1912) periods. Out of his (Brahma) forehead issued forth Rudra (Shiva?), having a body that is half male and half female. Brahma instructed Rudra (Shiva) for the feminine side to separate from him and then start copulating and populating the earth. Rudra issued eleven females and elven males from his body, and they started having sex to populate the earth (*Padma Purana 2.1.3, The Four Prominent Castes*). It seems that not only does Rudra (Shiva) have a feminine side but that Brahma also had a feminine side as in *Ramayana Book 6, Yuddha Kand 22, The Sons of Ravana.*

Shiva had sex with himself! Shiva and Brahma are what you call hermaphrodites or echinoderms like earthworms, snails, and starfish. So therefore, there is no problem at all in portraying Shiva or Avalokiteshvara as a god or goddess. In Japan, Guanyin is pronounced as Kwannon and Kan'on, or more formally as Kanzeon. This rendition was used for an earlier spelling for the well-known Canon manufacturer, which is a name for Chinese Buddhist Guanyin and the Hindu Shiva.

Shiva is the Hindu god, a destroyer of evil and part of the Hindu trimuti (Brahma and Vishnu). In Shaivism tradition, Shiva is a supreme being who creates, protects, and transforms the universe. The worship of the Moon god, "Sin," was a dominant religion of the Sumerian, Babylonian, and Assyrians. The insignia of the Moon god, Sin, looked like that of the Hindu god Shiva. Shiva is also known as Somnath, which means "Lord of the Moon," and Shiva's insignia has a crescent moon and the bull called "Vrishabha" or "Nandi," which was the vehicle of the Shiva.

There are Dagon, Oannes, Matsyavatar of Vishnu, and Nara Meru (all fish gods from different places). For example, Dagon is a god of fish, god of crop fertility, and can be seen in stone sculptures as part man-fish.

Indra is a very popular deity in Buddhism, who protects Buddhist teachings and believers and is commonly found in Theravada and Mahayana in Southeast Asia. In Buddhism, Indra is known as Sakra or Sakka. He also appears in ancient Buddhist text and literature as a deity that urges Gautama to teach mankind after he had received his enlightenment. In China, he is known as Pinyin, Shi Do Huan Yin; Korea: Je-Seok Cheon or Hwan-in; Japanese: Tai Shaku-Ten. In Japan, Indra always appear beside Brahma (Broten).

Mitra or Maitreya (Samskrit) is the same as Metteyya in the Buddhist Pali Canon and is regarded as the future Buddha of this world and is expected to appear on earth in the future. The Maitreya will be the successor of the present Buddha or Gautama Siddhartha.

Child sacrifices were practiced by the Canaanites offering children to the fire god Moloch, and you can find similar evidences in carving of the Vedic (Hindu) goddess, Kali, in tantric traditions with four hands carrying weapons, wearing a garland of skulls around her neck, and suppressing a child in an act of sacrifice. The Canaanite goddess Astarte can also be seen in a picture sitting and below her feet are skull. She holds two snakes high over the head of two horses, similar to that of Kaali! The equivalent of Kaali in Tibetan Buddhism is called Troma Nagmo, which means "Black Fierce Mother" and is a key practice in the Nyingma and Dzogchen traditions of Indo-Tibetan Buddhism. Even though child sacrifice is not practiced today, the deity is still worshipped this very day.

Ishtar is the Babylonian and Assyrian goddess of fertility, war, love, and sex and is the counter part of the Sumerian Inanna and is a cognate of the Northwest Semitic goddess Astarte. This is equivalent to Hariti, the goddess of fertility in Buddhism, which is part of Avalokiteshvara. The Vedic god, a carrier of Vishnu, is Garuda, which is represented by the head of a bird (eagle or falcon) with a human body and has been represented in many puranas (is the Hindu Vedic Text describing the creation of the universe and stories of gods, demigods) as a warrior who killed serpents. The carving of the Garuda can be seen in the stone carvings in Egypt, Cambodia, and also represented in the Hindu practices in Indonesia.

The intent of the above section on ancient gods and deities is not to list every ancient deity of the Matanni, Hittite, Hurrian, Canaanite, and Sumerian, etc. civilization. The intent is to show that the gods and deities from the Matanni, Hurrian, Hittite, Sumerian, Canaanite did not disappear into oblivion but migrated into India and Southeast Asia. The source of the English word *Aryan* comes from the Sanskrit Arya. Used by the Vedic Indic people who migrated into the Indian subcontinent about 1500 BCE. They brought their influences by the Matanni, Hittite, Canaanite, Hurrian, and Sumerian, etc. culture, language, religious beliefs and worshipped to the Indus Valley civilization. The influences of Hinduism and Buddhism were so great that it spread to the whole of India and later to the whole of Southeast Asia. This is to show that ancient gods and idols are alive and thriving. So what you see practiced today is akin to what were practiced in the past!

The conclusion is that the worship of the ancient gods and idols by millions are alive and well in many parts of the world and that Hinduism and Buddhism, except for Theravada Buddhism, are the vehicle in which it is thriving. Certainly, if more research is conducted, it is possible to link up more of gods and idols of the Hurrian, Matanni, Hittite, Sumerian, and Canaanite civilization and its movement to India and Southeast Asia, but that is not the main objective in this writing. You can find that addressed in my book *Hinduism and the Man on the Cross*.

GAUTAMA SIDDHARTHA

Gautama Siddhartha experienced and saw all the pain and suffering around him and sought to find an answer and solution to the problems. The noble Gautama Siddhartha was very insightful and recognized that mankind had been beset by the "curse of sin" (a biblical terminology) and death with no escape, and he went about trying to set himself free and arrived at his own conclusions with influences from the Hindu environment that he grew up. Gautama Siddhartha spent countless hours in meditation; he supposedly was able to suppress all his desires, lust, cravings, greed, wants, and needs and escaped from the *Samsara cycle of this life, therefore achieving Buddhahood. *Therefore, Gautama Siddhartha's or the Buddha's definition of Happiness is the cessation of all wants, lusts, greed, cravings, and needs! This is similar to the Hindu doctrine on *Self-Realization or in unity with the "Atman" or Universal Spirit, which is a foreign spiritual entity with many different names, like Braham, Krishna, Vishnu, etc.*

The keystone to a Buddhist's beliefs is the cessation of all desires, lusts, wants, and needs is through the practice of meditation. This basic fundamental belief forms the basis for Buddhism. In order to be able to achieve all cessation of desire, lusts, cravings, greed, wants, and needs, Gautama Buddha Siddhartha introduced to his followers the Four Noble Truths and the Eightfold Path or Golden Rules. Buddhism developed more, and more steps in the hundreds, and steps within steps are introduced by monks from different orders, sects, or schools in order to teach the general public and followers on how to achieve *enlightenment* or Nirvana, which is the same as the Hindu doctrine of *Self-Realization in a consistent and logical manner.

The other part of Buddhism's core belief is in the *Samsara cycle. It is differentiated from the Hindu Samsara in that the Hindu version, the same person is reincarnated into whatever it deserved from the merits and demerits accumulated. Whereas in Buddhism, the person is a non-self, and therefore continually changing and is rebirthed into another non-self. It is a very difficult Eastern concept to grasp. And where that non-self is rebirthed depends on the demerits and merits accumulated over a lifetime. Read some more on the Samsara cycle under section 7 fundamental Buddhist doctrines and in the ancient sacred Vedic Hindu texts references in chapter 35.

3

Beginning of Christianity (~2000 BC)

A supreme being (God), the creator of the heavens and earth and mankind, appeared to a man named Abraham in *Ur of the Chaldeans*, which is Iraq of this present day, and promised Abraham that if he worships only Him, the One and only true God and leave his home country, God will give him land much greater than the present-day Israel, that he will have many descendants as the stars in the heavens and a son, and through this specific son, all the nations in the world will be blessed. That is the beginning of Christianity. Jesus Christ, through the bloodline of Abraham and King David, was the declared Son of God. Through Jesus's death on the cross and resurrection, He was able to defeat sin and death and give eternal life to those that believe in Him, and therefore blessed all the people from the different nations. The Bible traced the birth of Jesus Christ all the way back to Abraham. There are hundreds of prophecies or foretelling by the ancient prophets of the coming of Jesus Christ the Messiah, as well as His birth, death, and resurrection.

4

Types of Buddhism

The pure form of teachings and practices of Gautama Siddhartha is regarded as Theravada Buddhism. Out of Theravada Buddhism (Sri Lanka and Southeast Asia) grew Mahayana (the greater vehicle found in East Asia) five hundred years later, and then Hinayana Buddhism (Lesser Vehicle), Vajrayana Buddhism (Tibetan), Zen Buddhism (Japanese), and many other schools of Buddhism. Out of the four basic types of Buddhism grew many variations according to cultures, locations, and superstitions of the different areas or locations. Theravada and Mahayana Buddhism are different expressions of the same teaching of Gautama Siddhartha as they do agree on the basic practices and doctrines. Even as there are disagreements and schisms over monastic instructions, interpretations, and expressions, they do get along. Essentially, all forms of Buddhism practice activities that yield merits like teachings, prostrations, offerings, prayers, and acts of kindness and compassion (to earn merits) with the realization that it is through meditation on the different stages of the path of renunciation that is necessary to attain *enlightenment or *Self-Realization and the wisdom of achieving emptiness.

A. Theravada Buddhism

Theravada Buddhism is characterized by its exploration and coming to understanding human nature and is focused on a *meditative approach to the transformation of a person. A follower of Theravada Buddhism is asked to abstain from all kinds of *evil*, accumulate merits by doing good, and to meditate in order to suppress all forms of cravings, wants, lusts, greed that rise from within until it rises no more. However, Buddhism does not define or list what *all those evils* are, whereas it does in Christianity as it is found in the laws, statutes, and ordinances. Once the follower is successful in suppressing all his or her cravings, lusts, desires, wants, and needs and accumulated sufficient merit points, he or she is regarded to have become a Buddha and, upon death, will escape the *Samsara cycle of rebirth and, therefore, attain Nirvana.

B. Mahayana Buddhism

Mahayana Buddhism is known as the *Greater Vehicle* and its fundamental teaching is a person can achieve Nirvana or *Self-Realization or become a Buddha only through complete trust in the Amitabha. Amitabha means *Infinite Light* or *The Buddha of Immeasurable Life and Light*. The Amitabha is said to be a former king, Dharmakara, who became a Buddhist and achieved Bodhisattva through his resolutions expressed in his forty-eight vows and sutras (teachings). A Bodhisattva is a person who is one stage short of attaining Nirvana or Buddhahood or had decided to delay it and stayed around to assist others to attain Nirvana or become a Buddha. The Amitabha is identified as the red Buddha. The different schools of Buddhism that falls under Mahayana Buddhism are (a) Tantra school (yoga), (b) the Pure Land sect practiced in Nepal and Tibet, and (c) Ch'an and Zen Buddhism practiced in China and Japan respectively.

C. Hinayana Buddhism

Hinayana is known as the *Lesser Vehicle*, and because of the negative connotation of the term, the World Fellowship of Buddhists decided that the term should be dropped to refer to Buddhism existing today and just be referred as Theravada Buddhism.

There are many schools or sects of Buddhism, and what this means is that each school or sect defines its own route and emphasis or interpretations on how to attain Nirvana or Bodhisattva. However, the main fundamental doctrines with regards to the Samsara cycle, the Four Noble Truths, and the *Eightfold Path do not change. Regardless, if the *Samsara cycle, which is the *core doctrine* for all schools and sects of Buddhism falls apart, then all is in vain.

D. Vajrayana Buddhism

Vajrayana Buddhism can be traced to wandering Yogis in Northern India known for their tantric meditations, which is reputed to be the superior form of meditation and tantric rituals, which leads to a faster vehicle to liberation from the Samsara cycle. Vajrayana is normally translated as the *Thunderbolt Vehicle*, referring to the mythical weapon which is also used as a ritual implement. It also embodies the concepts of ascended immortals or deities, and believers are asked to focus on a deity for their tantric ritual. Vajrayana Buddhism also teaches that the transmission of certain teachings cannot be done, except if it occurs directly from teacher to student during empowerment sessions, which makes it very exclusive and controlling.

E. Chinese Buddhism

It is generally agreed that Buddhism arrived in China after 190 BC, through Buddhist monks from India and when the Indian Mahayana text or sutras were translated into Chinese. At that time, China was already practicing some form of worship of ascended mortal deities, who had achieved immortality and proceeded to incorporate Buddhism into its beliefs. It was further influenced by the teachings of a revered philosopher, Lao Tze. This gave birth to Taoist Buddhism with its belief in pantheons of ascended deities or immortals that the believers revered even until today with its worship and offerings to ascended immortals for protection, safety, and prosperity. So this practice of Buddhist Taoism is practiced throughout Southeast Asia today. Many of the followers today are only going through the motions with its ceremonies and rites without truly understanding or questioning the roots and basis of their beliefs.

F. Tibetan Buddhism

Tibetan Buddhism is a mixture of Chinese Buddhism, Mahayana, and Vajrayana Buddhism. Tibetan Buddhism teaches methods which it believes allow its believers to become a Buddha and achieve Nirvana or Bodhisattva more quickly by including tantric meditations, which is similar to the *Yogic meditation and its mantrams, with its practices to accompany the Mahayana paths with the intention to become enlightened for the sake of all its followers. A Tibetan Buddhist teacher is a lama. Tibetan Book of the Dead lays out the stages a person goes through while dying, while dead, and then as they are being prepared for rebirths (i.e., the workings of the *Samsara cycle). During each stage, the appropriate texts are read to the dead, and if the dead hears and understands the true meaning, they will attain Nirvana or Unity with the Atman, Universal spirit or foreign entity, without being reborn.

G. Zen Buddhism (Japanese)

Buddhism was introduced into Japan around AD 552 by Buddhist monks from Korea. But some sources said they felt that Chinese Buddhism had a major contribution around AD 250–540. There are different Buddhist schools of thought, and here are some of them: Pure Land Buddhism, Nichiren Buddhism, Shinto Buddhism, and Zen Buddhism. The fundamental doctrine and ideology remains the same, but the pathways to achieving Nirvana can be different according to the teaching of the head monk of the school or temple.

H. Indian Buddhism

Indian Buddhism believes in afterlife and Moksha, akin to Nirvana, and is greatly influenced by Hinduism, similarly Chinese Buddhism by Taoism and Confucianism. Moksha in Hinduism refers to the liberation from the cycle of birth and death, as human life is believed to be full of suffering and pain. Indian Buddhism does not believe in non-self-doctrines and has a major emphasis on its own form of meditation. The types of Buddhism practiced in India are mostly Theravada and Vajrayana Buddhism.

5

Types of Christianity

There are many different Protestant and Evangelical Christian groups, like Pentecostals, Baptists, Anglican, Lutheran, United, Methodists, etc., as well as independent community churches, home churches, and groups or individual followers of Jesus. There are also the Greek Orthodox, Eastern Orthodox Churches, etc. Many of the churches are set up like *franchises*. There are also many different and very large Christian sects, or sometimes referred to as cults, like Roman Catholicism, Mormonism, Jehovah's Witnesses, Two by Two(s), etc. There are many who call themselves Christians and are not. A Christian cult is defined as a group of people whose many practices are not found or are contrary to what is written in the Bible, and in many instances, they are very authoritarian or even dictatorial. That does not mean that there are no Christians believers in them at all. Christianity is no different than Buddhism in that if any group elected to believe differently, they just break off from the main group and form their own groups. Roman Catholicism added seven more books that they felt should be in the Bible (sixty-six books) and then deemed that the total of seventy-three books inadequate, and therefore wrote their own catechisms, liturgies, and practices to complement their own bible. The Roman Catholic Church referred to them as Sacred Mysteries associated with the historical church traditions.

6

Beliefs and Definitions

A. Basic Buddhist Belief

Man must save himself because no one will save him. Man can only save himself through meditation and following the Eightfold Path and the Four Noble Truths as established by Gautama Siddhartha. He supposedly was successful and had achieved Nirvana in that he was able to overcome all forms of cravings, lusts, greed, wants, and needs. Today, there are many Buddhist schools of thoughts, teachings, and practices, and therefore they all promote different pathways to achieve Nirvana. For some, there are hundreds of steps for all the different levels of being a Buddhist, especially for those who are monks and nuns aspiring to be a Buddha or Bodhisattva.

B. Basic Christian Belief

A sinful man cannot save himself and needs God's help, which comes in the way of His Son Jesus Christ, as there is no other way whereby man can be saved. In this case, Jesus Christ is the life jacket or life raft.

The foundational and core belief of the Christian faith is that Jesus is the Begotten Son of God, who was sacrificed on the cross for the sins of the world, and that He resurrected from the dead. If a person accepts the work of Jesus Christ, the Son of God, on the cross and His resurrection, then this person is called a born-again person. He or she is born of the Spirit of God, in that the Spirit of God now dwells or lives in that person. When that happens, the person inherits eternal life, and therefore, he or she will be resurrected from the dead. This basic belief is based on the Gospel of John 3:16, "For God so loved the world that He gave His Only Begotten Son that whosoever believes in Him shall not perish but have everlasting life."

Similar to Buddhism, if any part of the core belief is proven false, then the whole of Christendom comes tumbling down, and all is vanity. In Christianity, the relationship and acceptance of God as a saviour is personal, and just because your parent(s) is a Christian does not make you one. Romans 8:2 sums up the basis for the purpose of Jesus on the Cross and His resurrection, and that is to set mankind free from "sin and death," that Gautama Siddhartha and mankind struggle with all his life and never coming free.

C. Happiness (Buddhism)

Gautama Siddhartha's or the Buddha's definition of *happiness* is the cessation of all lusts, cravings, greed, wants, and needs! Therefore, the keystone to a Buddhist's beliefs is cessation of all cravings, desires, lusts, wants, and needs, and it can be achieved through the practice of meditation. In order to achieve that, it usually takes more than a lifetime of training by meditation and strict discipline. Certain schools of Buddhism teach that they can achieve Nirvana within a lifetime through superior meditation techniques. So this leads us to the Buddhist belief in life's Samsara cycle, which is a vehicle for rebirth into this world. In Hinduism, achieving *Self-Realization means that one is totally free of all attachments, desires, lusts, wants, needs, etc., and when that happened, one is in full unity with god or the deity of Krishna, Brahma or Vishnu, etc. (i.e., one is infilled with a foreign spirit or entity). In other words, it is spiritual possession by a foreign spirit or entity.

D. Blessed (Christianity) as Compared to Happiness

To be blessed is to find favour with God, and it comes in many ways, like safety, family, peace, satisfaction, being in the presence of God, gift of wisdom, protection from one's enemies, etc. Listed below are just a few of the examples of those who are blessed by God:

Psalm 1:1(~1035–961 BC) says, "How blessed is the man who does not walk in the counsel of the wicked, Nor stand in the path of sinners, Nor sit in the seat of scoffers!"

Psalm 41:2 says, "The Lord will protect him and keep him alive, And he shall be called blessed upon the earth; And do not give him over to the desire of his enemies."

Psalm 84:5 says, "How blessed is the man whose strength is in You, In whose heart are the highways to Zion!"

Psalm 84:12 says, "O Lord of hosts, How blessed is the man who trusts in You!"

Psalm 89:15 says, "How blessed are the people who know the joyful sound! O Lord, they walk in the light of Your countenance."

Psalm 128:4 says, "Behold, for thus shall the man be blessed Who fears the Lord."

7

Fundamental Buddhist Doctrines

A. Buddhist *Samsara Cycle

Gautama Siddhartha was greatly influenced by the Hindu concept of the Samara cycle, which is a mechanism or system of reincarnation. However, Gautama Siddhartha arrived at his own version of reincarnation and called it rebirth. The reason it is called rebirth is because Buddhists believe in non-self (anatta [Pali] or Anatman [Sanskrit]), where the non-self continually changes due to the environment and people exposure and influence in every second of the day. Therefore, the non-self (Anatta) is not the same person as he or she was a few seconds ago, so a person that is rebirthed from the *Samsara cycle is different from the person that is coming out of the Samsara cycle.

The Buddhist believes in the following:

(i)   When a person dies, he or she enters the *Samsara cycle of life.

(ii) By doing good, he or she accumulates merits and that elevates him/her in the Samsara cycle versus doing bad, evil thoughts, etc., which will demote him/her in the Samsara cycle of life.

(iii) The degree to which they are able to suppress his desire, wants, needs, cravings, lusts, greed will also affect the level that he/she ends up in the Samsara cycle.

(iv) It is only when a person reaches perfection or Nirvana, where there is absence of desire, wants, needs, cravings, lusts, greed, evil thoughts, and accompanied by doing good, then he/she will attain or become a Buddha and be free of the Samsara cycle, thus Nirvana; and

(v) when a person attains or becomes a Buddha, he/she is free of the Samsara cycle, and sometimes this *cycle of life* may take several hundreds of years before one is free of it. So the level of his or her existence on this earth at the present moment depends on his/her performance in the past life!

Comments: Heaven forbid that one should do something bad and enter the Samsara cycle and come back to life as an earthworm. So the question is, how is the earthworm going to do good and redeem itself to get back to its former self, at the least? All the earthworm does is eat the earth, and how it is going to perform good works and obtain sufficient merits become a major problem for anyone to resolve. Possibly, the Samsara cycle has a secret way of evaluating merits and demerits for earthworms, but no one knows for certain, not even Buddha. How about all those good and bad bacteria, microbes, and viruses, how are they going to accumulate good merits points, and who is keeping the scores? The sheer immensity of keeping track of all the merits and demerits of bacteria, viruses, and microbes is mind-boggling, much less keeping track of humans which only makes up for nine billion in the world today? The intent of the questions here is not to ridicule a faith but to put forth honest questions with a pure heart that a person needs answers to in order to find out more about the Buddhist faith. And that is true with all the subsequent questions in this book. Buddhism, different from Hinduism, does not tell you who is responsible and operates the Samsara cycle.

B. Hindu *Samsara Cycle

The basic difference with the Hindu belief with regard to the *Samsara cycle is that Hindus believe that there is a self or human soul, and that it does not change but remains the same through the Samsara cycle, thus reincarnation. Hindus also believe that they will come back from the Samsara cycle depending on the same system of merits and demerits, but that their return is a reincarnation. But the same problem exists as to how, if he comes back as an earthworm, (devolved) is the earthworm going to earn sufficient merits and come back higher in the Samsara cycle of life and those with the lack of merit will be devolved. The deity Krishna claimed that he is responsible for the total operation of the Samsara cycle.

C. Questions on the Samsara Cycle

Q1. When the earth first came into existence, where does the first life come from, the Samsara cycle? If so, it means the Samsara cycle is capable of generating new lives that are nonexistent previously.

Q2. If the answer to Q1 is from the Samsara cycle, how then does the population multiply without coming from the Samsara cycle since all life must pass through the Samsara cycle?

Q3. When a person achieves Buddhahood and when he/she dies, where does he/she go to because he/she is no longer in the Samsara cycle?

Q4. How does or who in the Samsara cycle decides what level in the cycle a person goes to when he or she dies?

Q5. Today, there are some nine billion people in the world. The Samsara cycle is such a complex place, where and how is it able to take account of every good and bad that all the people of the world commit every second, minute, and hour of the day through their lifetime? Even the most complex computer in the world is unable to do that task, how then is the Samsara cycle able to do that, a memory of every good and bad deed of everyone that is born and the billions that had died previously over the thousands of years? And not only that but also to track every worm, insect, and sea life that ever existed and those that are here today?

Q6. How then does the worm, insect, bacteria, or sea life do good or bad in order to improve their station in the Samsara cycle?

Q7. Did this Samsara cycle come out of nowhere and suddenly introduce life through the cycle?

Q8. There are only a few Buddhist monks as compared to the number of Buddhists in the world. They do regard themselves as being superior because they are at a different level in the Samsara cycle, and the irony is they do beg for food once or twice a day from people who are at a lower cycle in the Samsara and subjected to all manner of desires, lusts, needs, greed, and have to toil for their food. Does it make any sense? Are the Buddhist monks a form of parasitic human lives that feeds of the labour of others who are lower in the Samsara cycle under the pretext that allows them to perform good deeds and accumulate merits?

Q9. When the solar system first came into existence, including the earth, there was no living organism at all. Therefore, at that time, was there a Samsara cycle? And if there was a Samsara cycle, then there is no life in it. Then if all life is rebirth, where did the first life come from the Samsara cycle? The earth, with its increasing and evolving living organisms, where does all the new lives come from?

Comments: If the Samsara cycle is a reality, then it means that people like Hitler, Stalin, Gen. Pol Pot, who had murdered millions, could slowly work themselves up the Samsara cycle by doing good works and accumulating merits. This also imply that to murder or take a life or lives is not all that horrendous, except for the victims because the murderer can always work his or her way back up the Samsara cycle. What the Samsara cycle also means is that if a person commits multiple murders or rapes of children, he or she will just have to go further back in the cycle and spend a few lifetimes before getting back to where he or she was. That is a little price to pay for such a crime. The other rationale is that the person that is killed off gets a chance to start life over again by going through the cycle, and possibly a better life if he or she had accumulated sufficient merits. Furthermore, in the court of law and the justice system, a death sentence is no longer a deterrent at all for the crime. The reason for that is, the guilty party just goes a little further back in the Samsara cycle and will eventually work his or her way back up.

If the Samsara cycle does not work for the lowly earthworm, how then is the Samsara cycle valid for anyone of us? The whole key in Buddhism is the power of rebirths through the Samsara cycle, and if that does not work, then the whole basis for Buddhism collapses and comes to nothing. All that meditation, good works, and the Four Noble Truths and the Perfect Eightfold Path come to nothing.

D. Theravada Buddhism

Theravada teaches that enlightenment cannot be achieved in a single lifetime. Instead, one must break free the chains that bind mankind (shame, lust, cravings, hatred, greed) before being reborn and continue on the path of self-denial and meditation to eventual *enlightenment. Now this may take a few years or hundreds of years depending on the individual. Theravada Buddhism is totally atheistic, and therefore do not have a god, deity, or temple to worship, say prayers, or make offerings. All that a Theravada Buddhist does is spending his or her time in meditation. Some schools of Theravada Buddhism do practice a form of chanting or tantra Buddhism.

E. Mahayana Buddhism

Mahayana Buddhism teaches that some of those who attained Nirvana, which is the same as the *Self-Realization in Vedic Hinduism, had elected to stay around so that they can assist others to get out of or escape from the Samsara cycle, resulting in shortened stay in the Samsara cycle, possibly for just a lifetime. Some Mahayana Buddhists are undecided about if a person has a soul (self) or nonself, and therefore torn between the two ideologies, and like a true Buddhist, elect not to come to any conclusion. In some Mahayana and Taoist Buddhist traditions, they do have ascended human beings that had become immortals (*in unity with Krishna the Atman and be one as god) and had risen to the level of deities. Here, deities are not regarded as gods but just ascended immortals that have special attributes and powers. The believer will burn incense and offerings to the ascended immortals or deities for protection, safety, prosperity, blessings, etc.

F. Taoist Buddhism

Taoist Buddhism originated from and is practiced in Mainland China and was very popular, but after the communist's cultural revolution, there are very few practicing Taoists as compared to the size of the population. However, it is still popular in Taiwan and in Southeast Asia. Taoism has hundreds of deities or ascended immortals who had attained such status by being famous or well-known for their good works, and some are more popular than others. Here are some of the popular ones: (1) the Jade Emperor (Yu Huang), the highest deity; (2) Three Pure Ones: (a) Yu Ch'ing (Jade Purity), (b) Shang Ch'ing (Highest Purity), and (c) T'ai Ch'ing (Great Pure); (3) Queen of Heaven; and the list goes on and on. So Taoist Buddhist offers up prayers and burnt incense for blessings, protection, prosperity, and safety to all the different ascended immortals and deities with specific attributes for all the different aspects of their lives, as well as for their relatives who had passed away.

One of the common practices of Taoist Buddhists is to set on fire special pieces of paper to represent money, papier-mâché models of houses, cars, and even laptop computers so their dead can also enjoy modern-day conveniences. Others offer cooked food, fruits, cookies, and baked goods. However, the purveyors of such practices who are selling all these goods are nevertheless making oodles of money from such enterprises.

Comments: It is interesting to note that the Buddhists who carry on such traditional practices for generations do need to stop and ask some of the following questions to see if it still makes sense in today's society:

(i) Since I do not offer up food every day to the dead relatives, do they go hungry for several days and even months until my next offerings?

(ii) Now that the dead relatives have paper houses, do I need also need to offer up paper beds and pillows, blankets, or even microwave ovens for them to heat up their food?

(iii) How do the dead relatives know which burnt offerings are for them because there is no addresses or identification on the burnt offerings, or maybe that some other dead persons, whose relatives here on earth are poor and cannot offer up burnt offerings, got the burnt offerings instead?

(iv) Does a person have to offer up soap and shampoo, or the dead relatives will go unwashed for years?

(v) Does a dead person whose relative who do not offer burnt offerings have to go without those offerings and be sad and be depressed in the afterlife?

I know that the above questions sound like ridicule, but it is not. What I am saying is, if what you are doing is a reasonable practice, then how do you resolve some of the questions that arises?

G. Comments

Similarly, some Christian sects or cults also have ascended beings, and they are called *saints* where their believers would light candles to them and say prayers for safety, protection, blessings, etc. For example, Roman Catholics have their Saint Christopher, Mary, and Saint Jude, etc. However, in the scripture in the Bible, Apostle Paul wrote his epistle to the *saints in Ephesus*, and they could not possibly be dead. Otherwise, he would not be writing to them at all, and how could they possibly read his epistles? So in the Bible, there are no ascended mortals or immortals who receive worship or offerings. So the practice of worshipping ascended mortals or deities is a heresy, according to the Bible. Roman Catholicism has special requirement in order to qualify as saints, as well as rites and ceremonies to induct them into their hall of saints, thus granting them special and elevated status over their followers. Similar to the Taoists, some Christian sects or cults sell candles and indulgences for their moneymaking enterprises also. In the Christian Bible in 1 Corinthians 10:19–20 ("What do I mean then? That food sacrificed to idols is anything, or that an idol is anything? *No*, but *I say* that things which *the Gentiles* sacrifice, they sacrifice to demons and not to God; and I do not want you to become partners with demons. You cannot drink the cup of the Lord and the cup of demons; you cannot partake of the table of the Lord and the table of demons."), it says that the reality is that the food and drinks are offerings to demons.

H. Nirvana

Nirvana, the equivalent of Hindu doctrine of **Self-Realization, be one with the Atman or Universal Spirit, literally means blowing out or quenching and is part of the Dukkha (a Buddhist concept associated with suffering and pain, or an unsatisfactory condition) in the Four Noble Truths. It is identical to having achieved an empty state of the mind and heart so that it is a totally empty state of non-self. Buddhist scholars define the two states of Nirvana: one nirvana, when one is alive; and the other nirvana, when one is dead or the final nirvana. Nirvana** (*Enlightenment or *Self-Realization) in life is akin to one who is released from beliefs, cravings, desires, and suffering but still has a body, name, and life. Whereas nirvana afterdeath is nirvana without the body and is the complete cession of everything, including consciousness and rebirths. In Mahayana Buddhism, the highest form or level is not Nirvana, but those who continue to take rebirths to assist others and liberate them from the *Samsara cycle by teaching the Buddhist path, and that person is called a Bodhisattva.

However, according to Buddhism, what happens to a person who has reached Nirvana is a question that cannot be answered! That means there is no answer, as no one is able to come up with an answer! The reason for that is because they honestly do not know. All the thousands of hours are spent in meditation to deny the self of everything and finally to arrive at a place where no one really knows anything about. It just does not sound reasonable or even sane.

Some Buddhists believe that heaven is just a temporary place where those with sufficient merit points will enjoy sensual pleasure for a temporary period of time.

8

Fundamental Christian Doctrines: Paradise, a New Heaven, a New Earth, Death, Resurrection, and Judgment

A. Paradise

Luke 23:39–43 (~AD 30–74) says, "One of the criminals who were hanged there was hurling abuse at Him, saying, 'Are You not the Christ? Save Yourself and us!' But the other answered, and rebuking him said, 'Do you not even fear God, since you are under the same sentence of condemnation? And we indeed are suffering justly, for we are receiving what we deserve for our deeds; but this man has done nothing wrong.' And he was saying, 'Jesus, remember me when You come in Your kingdom!' And He said to him, 'Truly I say to you, *today you shall be with Me in Paradise.*'"

In *2 Corinthians 12:1–4 (~AD 64–66)*, it says, "Boasting is necessary, though it is not profitable; but I will go on to visions and revelations of the Lord. I know a man in Christ who fourteen years ago—whether in the body I do not know, or out of the body I do not know, God knows—such a man was caught up to the third heaven. And I know how such a man—whether in the body or apart from the body I do not know, God knows—*was caught up into Paradise* and heard inexpressible words, which a man is not permitted to speak."

Comments: When Jesus died on the cross, He went immediately to Paradise, and three days later, He was resurrected. From that, we can easily assume that it was a holding place for the dead. The person that went with Jesus did not automatically go to heaven or hell because judgment had not been passed, and that will be at Judgment Day (for more info go to page).

B. Prophecies: New Heaven and A New Earth

Isaiah 65:17–25 (Prophecy) (~740–698 BC) says,

> 'For behold, I create new heavens and a new earth; And the former things will not be remembered or come to mind. But be glad and rejoice forever in what I create; For behold, I create Jerusalem for rejoicing And her people for gladness. I will also rejoice in Jerusalem and be glad in My people; And there will no longer be heard in her The voice of weeping and the sound of crying. No longer will there be in it an infant who lives but a few days, Or an old man who does not live out his days; For the youth will die at the age of one hundred And the one who does not reach the age of one hundred Will be thought accursed. They will build houses and inhabit them; They will also plant vineyards and eat their fruit. They will not build and another inhabit, They will not plant and another eat; For as the lifetime of a tree, so will be the days of My people, And My chosen ones will wear out the work of their hands. They will not labor in vain, Or bear children for calamity; For they are the offspring of those blessed by the Lord, And their descendants with them. It will also come to pass that before they call, I will answer; and while they are still speaking, I will hear. The wolf and the lamb will graze together,

and the lion will eat straw like the ox; and dust will be the serpent's food. They will do no evil or harm in all My holy mountain,' says the Lord.

Isaiah 66:22 says, "'For just as the new heavens and the new earth, which I make will endure before Me,' declares the Lord, 'So your offspring and your name will endure.'"

Revelations 21:1–4 (~AD 90) says,

> Then I saw a new heaven and a new earth; for the first heaven and the first earth passed away, and there is no longer any sea. And I saw the holy city, new Jerusalem, coming down out of heaven from God, made ready as a bride adorned for her husband. And I heard a loud voice from the throne, saying, 'Behold, the tabernacle of God is among men, and He will dwell among them, and they shall be His people, and God Himself will be among them, and He will wipe away every tear from their eyes; and there will no longer be any death; there will no longer be any mourning, or crying, or pain; the first things have passed away.'

In 2 Peter 3:13 (~AD 30–67), it says, "But according to His promise we are looking for new heavens and a new earth, in which righteousness dwells."

Comments: According to prophecies, the Old Earth will be destroyed and passed away or renewed, and it is God's promise and intention to create a New Earth wherein people will live and the promise that there will no longer be any mourning, crying, or pain.

C. Heaven

Matthew 6:9–10 (~AD 30–60) says, "Pray, then, in this way: 'Our Father who is in heaven, Hallowed be Your name. Your kingdom come. Your will be done, On earth as it is in heaven.'"

Colossians 1:4–5 (~AD 62) says, "Since we heard of your faith in Christ Jesus and the love which you have for all the saints; because of the hope laid up for you in heaven, of which you previously heard in the word of truth, the gospel."

In 1 Peter 1:3–5 (~AD 30–67), it says, "Blessed be the God and Father of our Lord Jesus Christ, who according to His great mercy has caused us to be born again to a living hope through the resurrection of Jesus Christ from the dead, to obtain an inheritance which is imperishable and undefiled and will not fade away, reserved in heaven for you, who are protected by the power of God through faith for a salvation ready to be revealed in the last time."

Comments: Yes, heaven is an actual place as described in the Holy Scriptures!

In the Bible, there are sixty-six books regarded as the inspired Word of God written between 3500 BC to AD 90. It is a collection of books about the authority, power, and instructions of how God wants to fellowship with the people He had created. It is also a story of mercy, grace, miracles, redemption, and prophesies of things and of judgment that are to come. It is also God's way of telling you who and what He is, and that He has been around since before the beginning of time and will until the end of it. Look at what it has to say about the following.

D. Death

Psalm 146:4 says, "His (man's) spirit departs, he returns to the earth; In that very day his thoughts perish."

Ecclesiastes 9:4–6 (~937 BC) says, "For the living know they will die; but the dead do not know anything, nor have they any longer a reward, for their memory is forgotten. Indeed their love, their hate and their zeal have already perished, and they will no longer have a share in all that is done under the sun."

Ecclesiastes 12:6–7 says, "Remember Him before the silver cord is broken and the golden bowl is crushed, the pitcher by the well is shattered and the wheel at the cistern is crushed; then the dust will return to the earth as it was, and the spirit will return to God who gave it."

John 11:11–14 (~AD 30–90) says, "This He said, and after that He said to them, 'Our friend Lazarus has fallen asleep; but I go, so that I may awaken him out of sleep.' The disciples then said to Him, 'Lord, if he has fallen asleep, he will recover.' Now Jesus had spoken of his death, but they thought that He was speaking of literal sleep. So Jesus then said to them plainly, 'Lazarus is dead.'"

E. Resurrection (Risen from the Dead)

In 1 Corinthians 15:50–57 (~AD 54), it says,

> Now I say this, brethren, that flesh and blood cannot inherit the kingdom of God; nor does the perishable inherit the imperishable. Behold, I tell you a mystery; we will not all sleep, but we will all be changed, in a moment, in the twinkling of an eye, at the last trumpet; for the trumpet will sound, and the dead will be raised imperishable, and we will be changed. For this perishable must put on the imperishable, and this mortal must put on immortality. But when this perishable will have put on the imperishable, and this mortal will have put on immortality, then will come about the saying that is written, '*Death is swallowed up* in victory. *O death, where is your victory? O death, where is your sting?'* The sting of death is sin, and the power of sin is the law; but thanks be to God, who gives us the victory through our Lord Jesus Christ.

Clarification: The above passages are quoted from the holy scriptures (Bible) to show that when a person dies, he or she is asleep and awaits the resurrection of the purpose of judgment. Even though the body rots away, it does not enter the Samsara cycle.

Here, Jesus is talking about a day that is coming soon when, at the sound of the *trumpet from heaven,* all the dead will rise or be resurrected to face the *day of judgment.* Those who believed in Him (Jesus) will pass on to eternal life, but those who refused Him and His work on the cross are condemned. In this passage of scripture, it is the declaration of Jesus's victory over death by His resurrection.

In 1 Thessalonians 4:13–17 (~AD 51), it says,

> But we do not want you to be uninformed, brethren, about those who are asleep, so that you will not grieve as do the rest who have no hope. For if we believe that Jesus died and rose again, even so God will bring with Him those who have fallen asleep in Jesus. For this we say to you by the word of the Lord, that we, who are alive and remain until the coming of the Lord, will not precede those who have fallen asleep. For the Lord Himself will descend from heaven with a shout, with the voice of the archangel and with the trumpet of God, and the dead in Christ will rise first. Then we who are alive and remain will be caught up together with them in the clouds to meet the Lord in the air, and so we shall always be with the Lord. Therefore comfort one another with these words.

Clarification: This passage of scripture is describing the hope that is found in Jesus, who was resurrected from the dead that is available to all who believe in Him, and that He is coming for all His believers, dead and alive, at the sound of the trumpet in the day of judgment.

F. Resurrection with a New Body

Philippians 3:20–21 (~AD 49–51) says, "For our citizenship is in heaven, from which also we eagerly wait for a Saviour, the Lord

Jesus Christ; *who will transform the body of our humble state into conformity with the body of His glory, by the exertion of the power that He has even to subject all things to Himself."*

In *2 Corinthians 5:14–18 (~AD 57)*, it says,

> For the love of Christ controls us, having concluded this, that one died for all, therefore all died; and He died for all, so that they who live might no longer live for themselves, but for Him who died and rose again on their behalf. Therefore from now on we recognize no one according to the flesh; even though we have known Christ according to the flesh, yet now we know Him in this way no longer. *Therefore if anyone is in Christ, he is a new creature; the old things passed away; behold, new things have come.* Now all these things are from God, who reconciled us to Himself through Christ and gave us the ministry of reconciliation.

In *1 John 3:2–3 (~AD 30–90)*, it says, "Beloved, now we are children of God, and it has not appeared as yet what we will be. We know that when He appears, we will be like Him, because we will see Him just as He is. And everyone who has this hope fixed on Him purifies himself, just as He is pure."

In *1 Corinthians 15:42–54 (~AD 57)*, it says,

> So also is the resurrection of the dead. It is sown a perishable body, it is raised an imperishable body; it is sown in dishonour, it is raised in glory; it is sown in weakness, it is raised in power; it is sown a natural body, it is raised a spiritual body. If there is a natural body, there is also a spiritual body. So also it is written, "The first *man*, Adam, *became a living soul."* The last Adam became a life-giving spirit. However, the spiritual is not

first, but the natural; then the spiritual. The first man is from the earth, earthy; the second man is from heaven. As is the earthy, so also are those who are earthy; and as is the heavenly, so also are those who are heavenly. Just as we have borne the image of the earthy, we will also bear the image of the heavenly. Now I say this, brethren, that flesh and blood cannot inherit the kingdom of God; nor does the perishable inherit the imperishable. Behold, I tell you a mystery; we will not all sleep, but we will all be changed, in a moment, in the twinkling of an eye, at the last trumpet; for the trumpet will sound, and the dead will be raised imperishable, and we will be changed. For this perishable must put on the imperishable, and this mortal must put on immortality. But when this perishable will have put on the imperishable, and this mortal will have put on immortality, then will come about the saying that is written, *"death is swallowed up in victory. O death, where is your victory? O death, where is your sting?"* The sting of death is sin, and the power of sin is the law; but thanks be to God, who gives us the victory through our Lord Jesus Christ.

Comments: Much like the resurrected body of Jesus, all His believers will also inherit a new and glorious body that is incorruptible and has eternal life. According to the Holy Scriptures, mankind is not stuck in the Samsara cycle or is in never-never land (a place of fantasy or imagination), but those who believe in the Lord Jesus Christ will inherit a new and incorruptible body and dwell in New Earth.

G. Judgment

Hebrews 9:27–28 (~AD 64) says, "And inasmuch as it is appointed for men to die once and after this comes judgment, so

Christ also, having been offered once to bear the sins of many, will appear a second time for salvation without reference to sin, to those who eagerly await Him."

Clarification: This passage of scripture is telling you that Jesus Christ, the Saviour, will return to earth again to gather His believers, and the rest of those who believe not in Him to judgment and condemnation.

John 5:21–30 (~AD 30–90) says,

> For just as the Father raises the dead and gives them life, even so the Son also gives life to whom He wishes. For not even the Father judges anyone, but He has given all judgment to the Son, so that all will honour the Son, even as they honour the Father. He who does not honour the Son does not honour the Father who sent Him. Truly, truly, I say to you, he who hears My word, and believes Him who sent Me, has eternal life, and does not come into judgment, but has passed out of death into life. Truly, truly, I say to you, an hour is coming and now is, when the dead will hear the voice of the Son of God, and those who hear will live. For just as the Father has life in Himself, even so He gave to the Son also to have life in Himself; and He gave Him authority to execute judgment, because He is the Son of Man. Do not marvel at this; for an hour is coming, in which all who are in the tombs will hear His voice, and will come forth; those who did the good deeds to a resurrection of life, those who committed the evil deeds to a resurrection of judgment. I can do nothing on My own initiative. As I hear, I judge; and My judgment is just, because I do not seek My own will, but the will of Him who sent Me.

Clarification: Here, Jesus was saying that He, God the Son, had been given authority by God the Father and will be coming to judge all of mankind in the day of judgment. The major difference in here between those who believe in Jesus Christ and what He had done on the cross and those who do not is that they who believe, their sins are forgiven because of Jesus's sacrifice on the cross. Once God forgives us our sins, He will remember it no longer (Jeremiah 31:33–34 {~626 BC} says, "'But this is the covenant which I will make with the house of Israel after those days,' declares the Lord, 'I will put My law within them and on their heart I will write it; and I will be their God, and they shall be My people. They will not teach again, each man his neighbour and each man his brother, saying, *"Know the Lord," for they will all know Me, from the least of them to the greatest of them,' declares the Lord, 'for I will forgive their iniquity, and their sin I will remember no more."*). For those who do not believe, their names are not in God's Book of Life.

In 2 Corinthians 5:10 (~AD 57), it says, "For we must all appear before the judgment seat of Christ, so that each one may be recompensed for his deeds in the body, according to what he has done, whether good or bad."

Hebrews 9:27 (~AD 64) says, "And inasmuch as it is appointed for men to die once and after this comes judgment."

Revelations 14:6–7 (~AD 90) says, "And I saw another angel flying in mid-heaven, having an eternal gospel to preach to those who live on the earth, and to every nation and tribe and tongue and people and he said with a loud voice, 'Fear God, and give Him glory, because the hour of His judgment has come; worship Him who made the heaven and the earth and sea and springs of waters.'"

Clarification: In this passage of scripture (Revelations), the Apostle John in his exile on the island of Patmos had a heavenly vision where he spoke of judgment day for all.

The Book of Life and Second death

Psalm 69:28 (~1035–961 BC) says, "May they be blotted out of the book of life And may they not be recorded with the righteous."
Revelations 20:11–15 says,

> Then I saw a great white throne and Him who sat upon it, from whose presence earth and heaven fled away, and no place was found for them. And I saw the dead, the great and the small, standing before the throne, and books were opened; and another book was opened, which is the book of life; and the dead were judged from the things, which were written in the books, according to their deeds. And the sea gave up the dead, who were in it, and death and Hades gave up the dead, who were in them; and they were judged, every one of them according to their deeds. Then death and Hades were thrown into the lake of fire. *This is the second death, the lake of fire.* And if anyone's name was not found written in the book of life, he was thrown into the lake of fire.

Revelations 20:4–6 says,

> Then I saw thrones, and they sat on them, and judgment was given to them. And I saw the souls of those who had been beheaded because of their testimony of Jesus and because of the word of God, and those who had not worshiped the beast or his image, and had not received the mark on their forehead and on their hand; and they came to life and reigned with Christ for a thousand years. The rest of the dead did not come to life until the thousand years were completed. This is the first resurrection. Blessed and holy is the one who has a part in the first resurrection; over these the second death has no power, but they will be priests of God and of Christ and will reign with Him for a thousand years.

Revelations 21:6–8 says,

> Then He said to me, "It is done. I am the Alpha and the Omega, the beginning and the end. I will give to the one who thirsts from the spring of the water of life without cost. He who overcomes will inherit these things, and I will be his God and he will be My son. But for the cowardly and unbelieving and abominable and murderers and immoral persons and sorcerers and idolaters and all liars, their part will be in the lake that burns with fire and brimstone, which is the second death."

Clarification: Here, the holy scriptures are telling the reader that, after the judgment of God before His throne, those who did not accept the sacrifice of His Son on the cross and resurrection will be cast out into the fire and spend eternity there. Here, the Bible is also telling you that God is the beginning (Alpha, first letter of the alphabet, and Omega, the last letter of the alphabet; meaning, there is only one God and no one else).

9

Buddhist's Hell

There are many different Buddhist perspectives in the matter of hell. Gautama Siddhartha did not himself believe in a heaven or hell. However, as Buddhism spreads into many countries, it adopted many of the superstitions and/or mythologies of the areas where the believers are.

Some Buddhists regard hell as being stuck in the *Samsara cycle and continually reborn into this life of suffering, craving, lusts, desire, and greed here on earth and not being able to get out of the Samsara cycle. Hinduism preaches the same concept of hell. He continually desires to accumulate good merit points so that he can be set free and attain Nirvana, even though he has no knowledge of where or what it is. Some Buddhists also believe that hell is a temporary place where they are tortured before being returned to life on earth again, and that there is definitely no god behind heaven or hell.

Many of their beliefs depend on the superstitions and mythologies of land at the time of Buddhist influence. Some Buddhist groups, like Mahayana Buddhism, believe that there are some eight major hells and hundreds of subhells. There are different hells as a result of actions for killing, sexual depravity, intoxication, lying, heresy, sexual defilement, and premeditated killing of parents or of enlightened persons like a Bodhisattva. Some Buddhist groups believe there are deities or ascended immortals presiding over the different tortures prescribed for the person who died and is waiting for rebirths or the *Samsara cycle, which is found in Hinduism.

The grotesque tortures can range from being boiled, ripped apart by different implements, subjected to extreme temperatures or fire, being roasted in an oven, pierced with hot irons, sliced or chopped with an axe to repeated torments. The torture will go on until the karma is exhausted, that is, all the demerit points are used up before rebirths can happen or occur.

Others, like Buddhism in China and Southeast Asia believe in Diyu, the realm of the dead, as in Chinese mythology where there is a subterranean maze with different levels and chambers where souls of the dead are taken to atone for the sins or bad deed they had committed while they were alive. Some believe there are ten courts of hell, and others eighteen levels of hell where various forms of gruesome tortures are dished out until their *deaths,* after which they are restored to their original state, and then the tortures are repeated. Diyu is a hell that serves to punish and renew the spirit in preparation for rebirths. In Chinese mythology, the jade emperor put Yama in charge of overseeing the affairs of the Diyu with over twelve thousand hells located underneath the earth. There are some eight hells with cold tortures and eight with hot tortures, and thousands of other miscellaneous kinds of tortures imaginable. The concept of eighteen hells started in the Tang Dynasty where the Buddhist text, *Wen Diyu Jing,* mentioned over 130 worlds of hell but was simplified to eighteen for convenience.

So the concept of hell does vary widely in Buddhism, and there is no fixed text that they can agree on. That is very different from Christianity with its fixed biblical text.

10

Biblical Sheol, Hades, Pit, or Hell

Numbers 16:31–33 (~1645–1525 BC) says, "As he finished speaking all these words, the ground that was under them split open; and the earth opened its mouth and swallowed them up, and their households, and all the men who belonged to Korah with their possessions. So they and all that belonged to them went down alive to Sheol; and the earth closed over them, and they perished from the midst of the assembly."

Isaiah 38:18 (~750–698 BC) says, "For Sheol cannot thank You, Death cannot praise You; Those who go down to the pit cannot hope for Your faithfulness."

Revelations 9:1–2 (AD 90) says, "Then the fifth angel sounded, and I saw a star from heaven which had fallen to the earth; and the key of the bottomless pit was given to him. He opened the bottomless pit, and smoke went up out of the pit, like the smoke of a great furnace; and the sun and the air were darkened by the smoke of the pit."

Revelations 1:12–18 says,

> Then I turned to see the voice that was speaking with me. And having turned I saw seven golden lampstands; and in the middle of the lampstands I saw one like a son of man, clothed in a robe reaching to the feet, and girded across

His chest with a golden sash. His head and His hair were white like white wool, like snow; and His eyes were like a flame of fire. His feet were like burnished bronze, when it has been made to glow in a furnace, and His voice was like the sound of many waters. In His right hand He held seven stars, and out of His mouth came a sharp two-edged sword; and His face was like the sun shining in its strength. When I saw Him, I fell at His feet like a dead man. And He placed His right hand on me, saying, "Do not be afraid; I am the first and the last, and the living One; and I was dead, and behold, I am alive forevermore, and I have the keys of death and of Hades."

Revelations 20:13–15 says, "And the sea gave up the dead which were in it, and death and Hades gave up the dead which were in them; and they were judged, every one of them according to their deeds. Then death and Hades were thrown into the lake of fire. This is the second death, the lake of fire. And if anyone's name was not found written in the book of life, he was thrown into the lake of fire."

Mark 9:42–48 (~AD 70) says,

Whoever causes one of these little ones who believe to stumble, it would be better for him if, with a heavy millstone hung around his neck, he had been cast into the sea. If your hand causes you to stumble, cut it off; it is better for you to enter life crippled, than, having your two hands, to go into hell, into the unquenchable fire, where *their worm does not die, and the fire is not quenched.* If your foot causes you to stumble, cut it off; it is better for you to enter life lame, than, having your two feet, to be cast into hell, where *their worm does not die, and the fire is not quenched.* If your eye causes you to stumble, throw it out; it is better for you to enter the kingdom of God with one eye, than, having two eyes, to be cast into hell, where *their worm does not die, and the fire is not quenched.*

Luke 12:5 (~AD 30–74) says, "But I will warn you whom to fear: fear the One who, after He has killed, has authority to cast into hell; yes, I tell you, fear Him!"

In 2 Peter 2:4 (~AD 30–74), it says, "For if God did not spare angels when they sinned, but cast them into hell and committed them to pits of darkness, reserved for judgment."

In 2 Peter 3:7, it says, "But by His word the present heavens and earth are being reserved for fire, kept for the day of judgment and destruction of ungodly men."

11

The Hope in Jesus Christ

The Buddhist's only hope is to go through the Samsara cycle by continually doing more good than bad, and to move up the chain after being enlightened and be able to suppress all his or her cravings, desires, lusts, greed, power, etc. He or she finally escapes from the stronghold of the Samsara cycle and reaches Nirvana or Buddhahood, then where he or she goes to when death comes, the Buddhist does not really know. From the looks of it, there are very fewer and fewer Buddhist monks and nuns as compared to the ever-increasing world population. It is only logical to conclude that there are much less people getting enlightened, become a Buddha or a Bodhisattva, and therefore more and more people are getting stuck in the Samsara cycle. That is only considering humans on earth and without even considering all the other manners of life forms in the earth, in the sea, and in the air. Even after being in the Samsara cycle for hundreds of years, there is no guarantee of achieving Buddhahood!

There is a real dilemma for Buddhism in that the number of Buddhists and Buddhist monks or nuns are ever decreasing, and that the other population is growing by leaps and bounds. Does the Buddhist believe that nonbelievers have no choice but to go through the Samsara cycle? Further to that, no one is able to recollect that they are ever been tortured while going through the Samsara cycle before being rebirthed, and if that is the case, how is he or she going to learn from his or her past actions?

The major difference with Christianity is that Christianity guarantees a person *eternal life* the minute a person accepts Jesus Christ, the Son of God, who died on the cross for his or her sins, and that He was resurrected that all who believed in Him may have new life in him or her, and that the Holy Spirit (Spirit of God) comes and dwells in that person.

Buddhism believes that only man can save himself, whereas Christianity believes that a man cannot save himself and that God had to intervene because of His love for man by the sacrifice of His Begotten Son for sin.

Buddhism believes that the only way to deal with sin is to suppress it through meditation, whereas Christianity believes that through the death of Jesus on the cross, He dealt with sin by defeating sin at the root, thus overcoming sin and death by His resurrection. Therefore, sin has no longer any hold or control over the person, and that means that man can now be free and live by guidance of the Holy Spirit that now lives in him. Not that a Christian does not sin but that he or she is no longer a slave to sin and is able to exercise his freedom from sin by not obeying the call to sin. The Christian does not have to meditate in order to overcome sin in that he or she can choose or select to live by the Spirit, and therefore does not submit to sin.

Genesis 2:15–17 says, "Then the Lord God took the man and put him into the garden of Eden to cultivate it and keep it. The Lord God commanded the man, saying, 'From any tree of the garden you may eat freely; but from the tree of the knowledge of good and evil you shall not eat, for in the day that you eat from it you will surely die.'"

Genesis 3:1–24 (~1645–1525 BC) says,

> Now the serpent was more crafty than any beast of the field which the Lord God had made. And he said to the woman, "Indeed, has God said, 'You shall not eat from any tree of the garden?' The woman said to the serpent, 'From the fruit of the trees of the garden we may eat; but

from the fruit of the tree which is in the middle
of the garden, God has said, "You shall not eat
from it or touch it, or you will die." The serpent
said to the woman, "You surely will not die! For
God knows that in the day you eat from it your
eyes will be opened, and you will be like God,
knowing good and evil." When the woman saw
that the tree was good for food, and that it was
a delight to the eyes, and that the tree was desir-
able to make one wise, she took from its fruit and
ate; and she gave also to her husband with her,
and he ate. Then the eyes of both of them were
opened, and they knew that they were naked;
and they sewed fig leaves together and made
themselves loin coverings. They heard the sound
of the Lord God walking in the garden in the
cool of the day, and the man and his wife hid
themselves from the presence of the Lord God
among the trees of the garden. Then the Lord
God called to the man, and said to him, "Where
are you?" He said, "I heard the sound of You in
the garden, and I was afraid because I was naked;
so I hid myself." And He said, "Who told you
that you were naked? Have you eaten from the
tree of which I commanded you not to eat?" The
man said, "The woman whom You gave to be
with me, she gave me from the tree, and I ate."
Then the Lord God said to the woman, "What is
this you have done?" And the woman said, "The
serpent deceived me, and I ate." The Lord God
said to the serpent, "Because you have done this,
Cursed are you more than all cattle, And more
than every beast of the field; On your belly you
will go, And dust you will eat All the days of your
life; And I will put enmity Between you and the
woman, And between your seed and her seed; He

shall bruise you on the head, And you shall bruise him on the heel." To the woman He said, "I will greatly multiply Your pain in childbirth, In pain you will bring forth children; Yet your desire will be for your husband, And he will rule over you." Then to Adam He said, "Because you have listened to the voice of your wife, and have eaten from the tree about which I commanded you, saying, 'You shall not eat from it;' Cursed is the ground because of you; In toil you will eat of it All the days of your life. Both thorns and thistles it shall grow for you; And you will eat the plants of the field; By the sweat of your face You will eat bread, Till you return to the ground, Because from it you were taken; For you are dust, And to dust you shall return." Now the man called his wife's name Eve, because she was the mother of all the living. The Lord God made garments of skin for Adam and his wife, and clothed them. Then the Lord God said, "Behold, the man has become like one of Us, knowing good and evil; and now, he might stretch out his hand, and take also from the tree of life, and eat, and live forever"—therefore the Lord God sent him out from the garden of Eden, to cultivate the ground from which he was taken. So He drove the man out; and at the east of the garden of Eden He stationed the cherubim and the flaming sword which turned every direction to guard the way to the tree of life.

Comments: God created the man (Adam) and woman (Eve) from man. Sin came by Adam, the first man, when he disobeyed God knowingly, whereas Eve was deceived and sinned. Mankind continued to do evil in the sight of God, and God destroyed the world by a flood but saved only eight people (Noah and his family because Noah was faithful toward God) in a boat. So all mankind are descendants of Adam through Noah. In the study of Chinese word characters, it is discovered that the root meaning of the word *salvation* comes from the Chinese word character that represents eight people on a boat.

Genesis 6:9–18 says,

> These are the records of the generations of Noah. Noah was a righteous man, blameless in his time; Noah walked with God. Noah became the father of three sons: Shem, Ham, and Japheth. Now the earth was corrupt in the sight of God, and the earth was filled with violence. God looked on the earth, and behold, it was corrupt; for all flesh had corrupted their way upon the earth. Then God said to Noah, "The end of all flesh has come before Me; for the earth is filled with violence because of them; and behold, I am about to destroy them with the earth. Make for yourself an ark of gopher wood; you shall make the ark with rooms, and shall cover it inside and out with pitch. This is how you shall make it: the length of the ark three hundred cubits, its breadth fifty cubits, and its height thirty cubits. You shall make a window for the ark, and finish it to a cubit from the top; and set the door of the ark in the side of it; you shall make it with lower, second, and third decks. Behold, I, even I am bringing the flood of water upon the earth, to destroy all flesh in which is the breath of life, from under heaven; everything that is on the earth shall perish. But I will establish My covenant with you; and you shall enter the ark—you and your sons and your wife, and your sons' wives with you."

Clarification: One cubit is about eighteen inches or forty-six centimetres.

12

The Flood According to the Bible

Genesis 7:11–12 says, "In the six hundredth year of Noah's life, in the second month, on the seventeenth day of the month, on the same day all the fountains of the great deep burst open, and the floodgates of the sky were opened. The rain fell upon the earth for forty days and forty nights."

Genesis 7:21; 8:22 says,

> All flesh that moved on the earth perished, birds and cattle and beasts and every swarming thing that swarms upon the earth, and all mankind; of all that was on the dry land, all in whose nostrils was the breath of the spirit of life, died. Thus He blotted out every living thing that was upon the face of the land, from man to animals to creeping things and to birds of the sky, and they were blotted out from the earth; and only Noah was left, together with those that were with him in the ark. The water prevailed upon the earth one hundred and fifty days.

Genesis 8:1–21 says,

> But God remembered Noah and all the beasts and all the cattle that were with him in the

ark; and God caused a wind to pass over the earth, and the water subsided. Also the fountains of the deep and the floodgates of the sky were closed, and the rain from the sky was restrained; and the water receded steadily from the earth, and at the end of one hundred and fifty days the water decreased. In the seventh month, on the seventeenth day of the month, the ark rested upon the mountains of Ararat. The water decreased steadily until the tenth month; in the tenth month, on the first day of the month, the tops of the mountains became visible. Then it came about at the end of forty days, that Noah opened the window of the ark, which he had made; and he sent out a raven, and it flew here and there until the water was dried up from the earth. Then he sent out a dove from him, to see if the water was abated from the face of the land; but the dove found no resting place for the sole of her foot, so she returned to him into the ark, for the water was on the surface of all the earth. Then he put out his hand and took her, and brought her into the ark to himself. So he waited yet another seven days; and again he sent out the dove from the ark. The dove came to him toward evening and behold in her beak was a freshly picked olive leaf. So Noah knew that the water was abated from the earth. Then he waited yet another seven days, and sent out the dove; but she did not return to him again. Now it came about in the six hundred and first year, in the first month, on the first of the month, the water was dried up from the earth. Then Noah removed the covering of the ark, and looked, and behold, the surface of the ground was dried up. In the second month, on the twenty-seventh day of the month, the earth was dry. Then God spoke to Noah, saying, "Go out of the ark, you and your wife and your sons and your sons' wives with you. Bring out with you every living thing of all flesh that is with you, birds and animals and every creeping thing that creeps on the earth, that they may breed abundantly on the earth, and be fruitful and multiply on the earth." So Noah went out, and his sons and his wife and his sons' wives with him. Every beast, every creeping thing, and every bird, everything that moves on the earth, went out by their families from the ark. Then Noah built an altar to the Lord, and took of every clean animal and of every clean bird and offered burnt offerings on the altar. The Lord smelled the soothing aroma; and the Lord said to Himself, "I will never again curse the ground on account of man, for the intent of man's heart is evil from his youth; and I will never again destroy every living thing, as I have done. While the earth remains, Seedtime and harvest, And cold and heat, And summer and winter, And day and night Shall not cease."

Genesis 9:8–19 says,

Then God spoke to Noah and to his sons with him, saying, "Now behold, I Myself do establish My covenant with you, and with your descendants after you; and with every living creature that is with you, the birds, the cattle, and every beast of the earth with you; of all that comes out of the ark, even every beast of the earth. I establish My covenant with you; and all flesh shall never again be cut off by the water of the flood, neither shall there again be a flood to destroy the earth." God said, "This is the sign of the covenant which I am making between Me and you and every living creature that is with you, for all successive generations; I set My bow in the cloud, and it shall be for a sign of a covenant between Me and the earth. It shall come about, when I bring a cloud over the earth, that the bow will be seen in the cloud, and I will remember My covenant, which is between Me and you and every living creature of all flesh; and never again shall the water become a flood to destroy all flesh. When the bow is in the cloud, then I will look upon it, to remember the everlasting covenant between God and every living creature of all flesh that is on the earth." And God said to Noah, "This is the sign of the covenant which I have established between Me and all flesh that is on the *earth.*" Now the sons of Noah who came out of the ark were Shem and Ham and Japheth; and Ham was the father of Canaan. These three were the sons of Noah, and from these the whole earth was populated.

Comments: The population of the earth grew by leaps and bounds through Noah and his family. Out of Noah's descendants, God chose a man named Abraham elected to obey God. God promised that He will bless Abraham so that (1) his family will be as the stars in the heavens, (2) that God will give Abraham lots of land for his people (a land far greater than the existing borders of Israel), and (3) that through one specific *son* or *seed*, all the nations of the world will be blessed.

13

God's Promise and Covenant

A. God's Promise to Abraham

Genesis 22:15–18 says,

> Then the angel of the Lord called to
> Abraham a second time from heaven, and said,
> "By Myself I have sworn, declares the Lord,
> because you have done this thing and have not
> withheld your son, your only son, indeed I will
> greatly bless you, and I will greatly multiply your
> seed as the stars of the heavens and as the sand
> which is on the seashore; and your seed shall pos-
> sess the gate of their enemies. In your seed all the
> nations of the earth shall be blessed, because you
> have obeyed My voice."

Genesis 15:18 says, "On that day the Lord made a covenant with
Abram, saying, 'To your descendants I have given this land, from the
river of Egypt as far as the great river, the river Euphrates.'"

B. Confirmation of the Same Promised to Isaac (Abraham's Son)

Genesis 26:3–5 says,

> The lord appeared to him and said, "Do not go down to Egypt; stay in the land of which I shall tell you. Sojourn in this land and I will be with you and bless you, for to you and to your descendants I will give all these lands, and I will establish the oath, which I swore to your father Abraham. I will multiply your descendants as the stars of heaven, and will give your descendants all these lands; and by your descendants all the nations of the earth shall be blessed; because Abraham obeyed Me and kept My charge, My commandments, My statutes and My laws."

Clarification: The man, Abraham, was born in today's Iraq in the Ur of the Chaldeans around 1852–1872 BC, lived for 175 years, and died around 1677–1697 BC. Abraham lived a righteous life, and God called him out of Ur to the land of Canaan which God promised him and his descendants if he would follow and worship Him only.

C. Confirmation of the Same Promised to Jacob (Isaac's Son and Abraham's Grandson)

Genesis 28:11–15 says,

> He came to a certain place and spent the night there, because the sun had set; and he took one of the stones of the place and put it under his head, and lay down in that place. He had a dream, and behold, a ladder was set on the earth with its top reaching to heaven; and behold, the

angels of God were ascending and descending on it. And behold, the Lord stood above it and said, "I am the Lord, the God of your father Abraham and the God of Isaac; the land on which you lie, I will give it to you and to your descendants. Your descendants will also be like the dust of the earth, and you will spread out to the west and to the east and to the north and to the south; and in you and in your descendants shall all the families of the earth be blessed. Behold, I am with you and will keep you wherever you go, and will bring you back to this land; for I will not leave you until I have done what I have promised you."

Generations passed, and God gave the people of Israel His law, which is made up of His commandment, ordinances, and statutes through His prophet Moses. It is through this law that the people are able to know what is right or wrong before God. As a result of the law, the people knew what sins are before God. So you can see from here that people struggled with their wants, lusts, desires, greed, power, etc.

In order for them to be forgiven of their sins, God required a blood sacrifice. This is the part of His old covenant in which He promised the coming of the new covenant which he will establish.

14

An Example of a Sin Sacrifice as There Are Several and It Is Part of the Old Covenant

Leviticus 4:1–12 (~1445 BC) says,

> Then the Lord spoke to Moses, saying, "Speak to the sons of Israel, saying, 'If a person sins unintentionally in any of the things which the Lord has commanded not to be done, and commits any of them, if the anointed priest sins so as to bring guilt on the people, then let him offer to the Lord a bull without defect as a sin offering for the sin he has committed. He shall bring the bull to the doorway of the tent of meeting before the Lord, and he shall lay his hand on the head of the bull and slay the bull before the Lord. Then the anointed priest is to take some of the blood of the bull and bring it to the tent of meeting, and the priest shall dip his finger in the blood and sprinkle some of the blood seven times before the Lord, in front of the veil of the sanctuary. The priest shall also put some of the blood on the horns of the altar of fragrant incense which is

before the Lord in the tent of meeting; and all the blood of the bull he shall pour out at the base of the altar of burnt offering which is at the doorway of the tent of meeting. He shall remove from it all the fat of the bull of the sin offering: the fat that covers the entrails, and all the fat which is on the entrails, and the two kidneys with the fat that is on them, which is on the loins, and the lobe of the liver, which he shall remove with the kidneys (just as it is removed from the ox of the sacrifice of peace offerings), and the priest is to offer them up in smoke on the altar of burnt offering. But the hide of the bull and all its flesh with its head and its legs and its entrails and its refuse, that is, all the rest of the bull, he is to bring out to a clean place outside the camp where the ashes are poured out, and burn it on wood with fire; where the ashes are poured out it shall be burned."

15

There Is Nothing Else That God Will Accept for the Forgiveness of Sins

The First Passover

It is called *Passover* because the angel of death sent by God passed over the house of the Hebrew people because the doorposts had the blood of the lamb painted over it and killed all the firstborn of the Egyptians.

Leviticus 12:21–30 says,

> Then Moses called for all the elders of Israel and said to them, "Go and take for yourselves lambs according to your families, and slay the Passover lamb. You shall take a bunch of hyssop and dip it in the blood which is in the basin, and apply some of the blood that is in the basin to the lintel and the two doorposts; and none of you shall go outside the door of his house until morning. For the Lord will pass through to smite the Egyptians; and when He sees the blood on the lintel and on the two doorposts, the Lord will pass over the door and will not allow the destroyer to come in to your houses to smite you.

And you shall observe this event as an ordinance for you and your children forever. When you enter the land which the Lord will give you, as He has promised, you shall observe this rite. And when your children say to you, 'What does this rite mean to you?' you shall say, 'It is a Passover sacrifice to the Lord who passed over the houses of the sons of Israel in Egypt when He smote the Egyptians, instead of spared our homes.'" And the people bowed low and worshiped. Then the sons of Israel went and did so; just as the Lord had commanded Moses and Aaron, so they did. Now it came about at midnight that the Lord struck all the firstborn in the land of Egypt, from the firstborn of Pharaoh who sat on his throne to the firstborn of the captive who was in the dungeon, and all the firstborn of cattle. Pharaoh arose in the night, he and all his servants and all the Egyptians, and there was a great cry in Egypt, for there was no home where there was not some-one dead.

This Passover is an example to show that God will only accept a blood sacrifice as a covering and safety from His judgment. Several thousands of years have passed and God continued to establish His voice on earth through His Old Testament prophets, and in preserving the line of Abraham's seed through which His promise will be fulfilled. The testament of God is a testimony of His Words through the prophets, through miracles and prophesies.

It is through His prophets of old that He tells the people of a New Covenant to come, which is the fulfilment of the Old Covenant. The Old Covenant is a foreshadow of what is to come, and its fulfilment by Jesus, Son of God, the reality and New Covenant.

16

New Covenant

A. Prophecy and Promise of a New Covenant

Jeremiah 31:34 (~626 BC) says,

> "Behold, days are coming," declares the Lord, "when I will make a new covenant with the house of Israel and with the house of Judah, not like the covenant which I made with their fathers in the day I took them by the hand to bring them out of the land of Egypt, My covenant which they broke, although I was a husband to them," declares the Lord. "But this is the covenant which I will make with the house of Israel after those days," declares the Lord, "I will put My law within them and on their heart I will write it; and I will be their God, and they shall be My people. They will not teach again, each man his neighbour and each man his brother, saying, 'Know the Lord,' for they will all know Me, from the least of them to the greatest of them," declares the Lord, "for I will forgive their iniquity, and their sin I will remember no more."

B. Fulfilment of Prophecy

Luke 22:13–20 (~30–55 BC) says,

> And they left and found everything just as He had told them; and they prepared the Passover. When the hour had come, He reclined at the table, and the apostles with Him. And He said to them, "I have earnestly desired to eat this Passover with you before I suffer; for I say to you, I shall never again eat it until it is fulfilled in the kingdom of God." And when He had taken a cup and given thanks, He said, "Take this and share it among yourselves; for I say to you, I will not drink of the fruit of the vine from now on until the kingdom of God comes." And when He had taken some bread and given thanks, He broke it and gave it to them, saying, "This is My body which is given for you; do this in remembrance of Me." And in the same way He took the cup after they had eaten, saying, "This cup which is poured out for you is the new covenant in My blood."

C. Explanation of New Covenant

Hebrews 8:13–9:28 (~AD 64) says,

> When He said, "A new covenant," He has made the first obsolete. But whatever is becoming obsolete and growing old is ready to disappear. Now even the first covenant had regulations of divine worship and the earthly sanctuary. For there was a tabernacle prepared, the outer one, in which were the lampstand and the table and the sacred bread; this is called the holy place. Behind

the second veil there was a tabernacle which is
called the Holy of Holies, having a golden altar
of incense and the ark of the covenant covered
on all sides with gold, in which was a golden jar
holding the manna, and Aaron's rod which bud-
ded, and the tables of the covenant; and above it
were the cherubim of glory overshadowing the
mercy seat; but of these things we cannot now
speak in detail. Now when these things have been
so prepared, the priests are continually entering
the outer tabernacle performing the divine worship, but into the second, only the high priest
enters once a year, not without taking blood,
which he offers for himself and for the sins of
the people committed in ignorance. The Holy
Spirit is signifying this, that the way into the
holy place has not yet been disclosed while the
outer tabernacle is still standing, which is a symbol for the present time. Accordingly both gifts
and sacrifices are offered which cannot make the
worshiper perfect in conscience, since they relate
only to food and drink and various washings,
regulations for the body imposed until a time of
reformation. But when Christ appeared as a high
priest of the good things to come, He entered
through the greater and more perfect tabernacle,
not made with hands, that is to say, not of this
creation; and not through the blood of goats and
calves, but through His own blood, He entered
the holy place once for all, having obtained eternal redemption. For if the blood of goats and
bulls and the ashes of a heifer sprinkling those
who have been defiled sanctify for the cleansing
of the flesh, how much more will the blood of
Christ, who through the eternal Spirit offered
Himself without blemish to God, cleanse your

conscience from dead works to serve the living God? For this reason He is the mediator of a new covenant, so that, since a death has taken place for the redemption of the transgressions that were committed under the first covenant, those who have been called may receive the promise of the eternal inheritance. For where a covenant is, there must of necessity be the death of the one who made it. For a covenant is valid only when men are dead, for it is never in force while the one who made it lives. Therefore even the first covenant was not inaugurated without blood. For when every commandment had been spoken by Moses to all the people according to the Law, he took the blood of the calves and the goats, with water and scarlet wool and hyssop, and sprinkled both the book itself and all the people, saying, *"This is the blood of the covenant which god commanded you."* And in the same way he sprinkled both the tabernacle and all the vessels of the ministry with the blood. And according to the Law, one may almost say, all things are cleansed with blood, and without shedding of blood there is no forgiveness. Therefore it was necessary for the copies of the things in the heavens to be cleansed with these, but the heavenly things themselves with better sacrifices than these. For Christ did not enter a holy place made with hands, a mere copy of the true one, but into heaven itself, now to appear in the presence of God for us; nor was it that He would offer Himself often, as the high priest enters the holy place year by year with blood that is not his own. Otherwise, He would have needed to suffer often since the foundation of the world; but now once at the consummation of the ages He has been manifested to put away

73

sin by the sacrifice of Himself. And inasmuch as it is appointed for men to die once and after this comes judgment, so Christ also, having been offered once to bear the sins of many, will appear a second time for salvation without reference to sin, to those who eagerly await Him.

17

Some of the Prophecies in the Old Testament

A. Promise of a Messiah (A Saviour or Person to Save Mankind)

The Prophecy

(i) *Genesis 22:18* says, "In your seed all the nations of the earth shall be blessed, because you have obeyed My voice." *Clarification:* This is the promise of God to Abraham as written by Moses (~3,500 years ago).

(ii) *Micah 1:2–4 (~737–696 BC)* says, "'But as for you, Bethlehem Ephrathah, Too little to be among the clans of Judah, from you One will go forth for Me to be ruler in Israel. His goings forth are from long ago, From the days of eternity.' Therefore He will give them up until the time when she who is in labour has borne a child. Then the remainder of His brethren will return to the sons of Israel. And He will arise and shepherd His flock In the strength of the Lord, In the majesty of the name of the Lord His God. And they will remain, because at that time He will be great to the ends of the earth."

Fulfilment of the Prophecy

The prophetic fulfilment in Jesus Christ (the Messiah) whereby salvation and eternal life is available to all those who believe in him immediately, and there is no waiting to ascend the Samsara cycle or to be set free from the Samsara cycle.

John 3:16–18 (~30–AD 90) says, "For God so loved the world, that He gave His only begotten Son, that whoever believes in Him shall not perish, but have eternal life. For God did not send the Son into the world to judge the world, but that the world might be saved through Him. He who believes in Him is not judged; he who does not believe has been judged already, because he has not believed in the name of the only begotten Son of God."

Clarification: This is a promise and guarantee given by God that through His Son, Jesus Christ, you will receive eternal life if you believe in Him.

B. Forerunner for the Messiah

The Prophecy

(i) *Malachi 3:1 (~445 BC)* says, "'Behold, I am going to send My messenger, and he will clear the way before Me. And the Lord, whom you seek, will suddenly come to His temple; and the messenger of the covenant, in whom you delight, behold, He is coming,' says the Lord of hosts."

(ii) *Isaiah 40:3–5 (~740–698 BC)* says, "A voice is calling, 'Clear the way for the Lord in the wilderness; Make smooth in the desert a highway for our God.' Let every valley be lifted up, And every mountain and hill be made low; And let the rough ground become a plain, And the rugged terrain a broad valley; Then the glory of the Lord will be revealed, And all flesh will see it together; For the mouth of the Lord has spoken."

The Fulfilment of the Prophecy

Matthew 3:1–6 (~AD 60) says,

> Now in those days John the Baptist came, preaching in the wilderness of Judea, saying, "Repent, for the kingdom of heaven is at hand." For this is the one referred to by Isaiah the prophet when he said, *"The voice of one crying in the wilderness, 'Make ready the way of the lord, make his paths straight!'"* Now John himself had a garment of camel's hair and a leather belt around his waist; and his food was locusts and wild honey. Then Jerusalem was going out to him, and all Judea and all the district around the Jordan; and they were being baptized by him in the Jordan River, as they confessed their sins.

C. Virgin Birth (By Prophet Isaiah (~740–698 BC)

The Prophecy

Isaiah 7:14 (~740–698 BC) says, "Therefore the Lord Himself will give you a sign: Behold, a virgin will be with child and bear a son, and she will call His name Immanuel."

The Fulfilment of the Prophecy

Pronouncement by the Angel

(i) *Luke 1:26–38 (~AD 30–74)* says,

> Now in the sixth month the angel Gabriel was sent from God to a city in Galilee called Nazareth, to a virgin engaged to a man whose name was Joseph, of the descendants of David;

and the virgin's name was Mary. And coming in, he said to her, "Greetings, favoured one! The Lord is with you." But she was very perplexed at this statement, and kept pondering what kind of salutation this was. The angel said to her, "Do not be afraid, Mary; for you have found favour with God. And behold, you will conceive in your womb and bear a son, and you shall name Him Jesus. He will be great and will be called the Son of the Most High; and the Lord God will give Him the throne of His father David; and He will reign over the house of Jacob forever, and His kingdom will have no end." Mary said to the angel, "How can this be, since I am a virgin?" The angel answered and said to her, "The Holy Spirit will come upon you, and the power of the Most High will overshadow you; and for that reason the holy Child shall be called the Son of God. And behold, even your relative Elizabeth has also conceived a son in her old age; and she who was called barren is now in her sixth month. For nothing will be impossible with God." And Mary said, "Behold, the bond slave of the Lord; may it be done to me according to your word.' And the angel departed from her."

(ii) *Matthew 1:18–23 (~AD 60)* says,

Now the birth of Jesus Christ was as follows: when His mother Mary had been betrothed to Joseph, before they came together she was found to be with child by the Holy Spirit. And Joseph her husband, being a righteous man and not wanting to disgrace her, planned to send her away secretly. But when he had considered this, behold, an angel of the Lord appeared to him in a dream, saying, "Joseph, son of David, do not be afraid to take Mary as your wife; for the Child who has been conceived in her is of the Holy Spirit. She will bear a Son; and you shall call His name Jesus, for He will save His people from their sins." Now all this took place to fulfill what was spoken by the Lord through the prophet: "Behold, the virgin shall be with child and shall bear a son, and they shall call his name Immanuel," which translated means, "God with us."

(iii) The Birth of Jesus. *Luke 2:1–19 (~AD 30–74)* says,

Now in those days a decree went out from Caesar Augustus, that a census be taken of all the inhabited earth. This was the first census taken while Quirinius was governor of Syria. And everyone was on his way to register for the census, each to his own city. Joseph also went up from Galilee, from the city of Nazareth, to Judea, to the city of David, which is called Bethlehem, because he was of the house and family of David, in order to register along with Mary, who was engaged to him, and was with child. While they were there, the days were completed for her to give birth. And she gave birth to her firstborn son; and she wrapped Him in cloths, and laid Him in a manger, because there was no room for them in the inn. In the same region there were some shepherds staying out in the fields and keeping watch over their flock by night. And an angel of the Lord suddenly stood before them, and the glory of the Lord shone around them; and they were terribly frightened. But the angel said to them, "Do not be afraid; for behold, I bring you good news of great joy which will be for all the people; for today in the city of David there has been born for you a Saviour, who is Christ the Lord. This will be a sign for you: you will find a baby wrapped in cloths and lying in a manger." And suddenly there appeared with the angel a multitude of the heavenly host praising God and saying, "Glory to God in the highest, And on earth peace among men with whom He is pleased." When the angels had gone away from them into heaven, the shepherds began saying to one another, "Let us go straight to Bethlehem then, and see this thing that has happened which the Lord has made known to us." So they came in a hurry and found their way to Mary and Joseph, and the baby as He lay in the manger. When they had seen this, they made known the statement, which had been told them about this Child. And all who heard it wondered at the things, which were told them by the shepherds. But Mary treasured all these things, pondering them in her heart.

D. Riding on a Colt

The Prophecy

Zechariah 9:9 (~520–480 BC) says, "Rejoice greatly, O daughter of Zion! Shout in triumph, O daughter of Jerusalem! Behold, your king is coming to you; He is just and endowed with salvation, Humble, and mounted on a donkey, Even on a colt, the foal of a donkey."

The Fulfilment of the Prophecy

Matthew 21:1–11 (~AD 60) says,

When they had approached Jerusalem and had come to Bethphage, at the Mount of Olives, then Jesus sent two disciples, saying to them, "Go into the village opposite you, and immediately you will find a donkey tied there and a colt with her; untie them and bring them to Me. If anyone says anything to you, you shall say, 'The Lord has need of them,' and immediately he will send them." This took place to fulfill what was spoken through the prophet: "*Say to the daughter of Zion, 'Behold your king is coming to you, gentle, and mounted on a donkey, even on a colt, the foal of a beast of burden.'*" The disciples went and did just as Jesus had instructed them, and brought the donkey and the colt, and laid their coats on them; and He sat on the coats. Most of the crowd spread their coats in the road, and others were cutting branches from the trees and spreading them in the road. The crowds going ahead of Him, and those who followed, were shouting, "Hosanna to the Son of David; *blessed is he who comes in the name of the Lord;* Hosanna in the highest!" When He had entered Jerusalem, all the city was stirred, saying, "Who is this?" And the crowds were saying, "This is the prophet Jesus, from Nazareth in Galilee."

E. Prophecy of the Trial and Crucifixion

(i) *Zechariah 12:10 (~520–480 BC)* says, "I will pour out on the house of David and on the inhabitants of Jerusalem, the Spirit of grace and of supplication, so that they will look on Me whom they have pierced; and they will mourn for Him, as one mourns for an only son, and they will weep bitterly over Him like the bitter weeping over a firstborn."

(ii) *Psalms 22:12–18 (~1035–961 BC)* says, "I am poured out like water, And all my bones are out of joint; My heart is like wax; It is melted within me. My strength is dried up like a potsherd, And my tongue cleaves to my jaws; And You lay me in the dust of death. For dogs have surrounded me; A band of evildoers has encompassed me; They pierced my hands and my feet. I can count all my bones. They look, they stare at me; They divide my garments among them, And for my clothing they cast lots."

The Fulfilment of the Prophecy

John 19:1–37 (~AD 33–90) says,

Pilate then took Jesus and scourged Him. And the soldiers twisted together a crown of thorns and put it on His head, and put a purple robe on Him; and they began to come up to Him and say, "Hail, King of the Jews!" and to give Him slaps in the face. Pilate came out again and said to them, "Behold, I am bringing Him out to you so that you may know that I find no guilt in Him." Jesus then came out, wearing the crown of thorns and the purple robe. Pilate said to them, "Behold, the Man!" So when the chief priests and the officers saw Him, they cried out saying, "Crucify, crucify!" Pilate said to them, "Take Him yourselves and crucify Him, for I find no guilt in Him." The Jews answered him, "We have a law, and by that law He ought to die because He made Himself out to be the Son of God." Therefore when Pilate heard this statement, he was even more afraid; and he entered into the Praetorium again and said to Jesus, "Where are You from?" But Jesus gave him no answer. So Pilate said to Him, "You do not speak to me? Do You not know that I have authority to release You, and I have authority to crucify You?" Jesus answered, "You would have no authority over Me, unless it had been given you from above; for this reason he who delivered Me to you has the greater sin." As a result of this Pilate made efforts to release Him, but the Jews cried out saying, "If you release this Man, you are no friend of Caesar; everyone who makes himself out to be a king opposes Caesar." Therefore when Pilate heard these words, he brought Jesus out, and sat down on the judgment seat at a place called The Pavement, but in Hebrew, Gabbatha. Now it was the day of preparation for the Passover; it was about the sixth hour. And he said to the Jews, "Behold, your King!" So they cried out, "Away with Him, away with Him, crucify Him!" Pilate said to them, "Shall I crucify your King?" The chief priests answered, "We have no king but Caesar." So he then handed Him over to them to be crucified. They took Jesus, therefore, and He went out, bearing His own cross, to the place called the Place of a Skull, which is called in Hebrew, Golgotha. There they crucified Him, and with Him two other men, one on either side, and Jesus in between. Pilate also wrote an inscription and put it on the cross. It was written, *"Jesus the Nazarene, the King of the Jews."* Therefore many of the Jews read this inscription, for the place where Jesus was crucified was near the city; and it was written in Hebrew, Latin and in Greek. So the chief priests of the Jews were saying to Pilate, "Do not write, 'The King of the Jews'; but that He said, "I am King of the Jews." Pilate answered, "What I have written I have written." Then the soldiers, when they had crucified Jesus, took His outer garments and made four parts, a part to every soldier and also the tunic; now the tunic was seamless, woven in one piece. So they said to one another, "Let us not tear it, but cast lots for it, to decide whose it shall be"; this was to fulfill the Scripture: *"they divided my outer garments among them, and for my clothing they cast lots."* Therefore the soldiers did these things. But standing by the cross of Jesus were His mother, and His mother's sister, Mary the wife of Clopas, and Mary Magdalene. When Jesus then saw His mother, and the disciple whom He loved standing nearby, He said to His mother, "Woman, behold, your son!" Then He said to the disciple, "Behold, your mother!" From that hour the disciple took her into his own household. After this, Jesus, knowing that all things had already been accomplished, to fulfill the Scripture, said, "I am thirsty." A jar full of sour wine was standing there; so they put a sponge full of the sour wine upon a branch of hyssop and brought it up to His mouth. Therefore when Jesus had received the sour wine, He said, "It is finished!" And He bowed His head and gave up His spirit. Then the Jews, because it was the day of preparation, so that the bodies would not remain on the cross on the Sabbath (for that Sabbath was a high day), asked Pilate that their legs might be broken, and that they might be taken away. So the soldiers came, and broke the legs of the first man and of the other who was crucified with Him; but coming to Jesus, when they saw that He was already dead, they did not break His legs. But one of the soldiers pierced His side with a spear, and immediately blood and water came out. And he who has seen has testified, and his testimony is true; and he knows that he is telling the truth, so that you also may believe. For these things came to pass to fulfill the Scripture, *"Not a bone of him shall be broken.*" And again another Scripture says, "They shall look on him whom they pierced."

F. The Prophecy of the Resurrection of Jesus from the Dead

Psalms 16:8–11 (~1035–961 BC) says, "I have set the Lord continually before me; Because He is at my right hand, I will not be shaken. Therefore my heart is glad and my glory rejoices; My flesh also will dwell securely. For You will not abandon my soul to Sheol (Hell); Nor will You allow Your Holy One to undergo decay. You will make known to me the path of life; In Your presence is fullness of joy; In Your right hand there are pleasures forever."

The Fulfilment of the Prophecy

Pronouncement by the Angels
Luke 24:1–12 (~AD 30–74) says,

> But on the first day of the week, at early dawn, they came to the tomb bringing the spices which they had prepared. And they found the stone rolled away from the tomb, but when they entered, they did not find the body of the Lord Jesus. While they were perplexed about this, behold, two men suddenly stood near them in dazzling clothing; and as the women were terrified and bowed their faces to the ground, the men said to them, "Why do you seek the living One among the dead? He is not here, but He has risen. Remember how He spoke to you while He was still in Galilee, saying that the Son of Man must be delivered into the hands of sinful men, and be crucified, and the third day rise again." And they remembered His words, and returned from the tomb and reported all these things to the

eleven and to all the rest. Now they were Mary Magdalene and Joanna and Mary the mother of James; also the other women with them were telling these things to the apostles. But these words appeared to them as nonsense, and they would not believe them. But Peter got up and ran to the tomb; stooping and looking in, he saw the linen wrappings only; and he went away to his home, marvelling at what had happened.

G. The Appearing of Jesus to His Followers

Luke 24:13–53 (~AD 30–74) says,

> And behold, two of them were going that very day to a village named Emmaus, which was about seven miles from Jerusalem. And they were talking with each other about all these things, which had taken place. While they were talking and discussing, Jesus Himself approached and began traveling with them. But their eyes were prevented from recognizing Him. And He said to them, "What are these words that you are exchanging with one another as you are walking?" And they stood still, looking sad. One of them, named Cleopas, answered and said to Him, "Are You the only one visiting Jerusalem and unaware of the things which have happened here in these days?" And He said to them, "What things?" And they said to Him, "The things about Jesus the Nazarene, who was a prophet mighty in deed and word in the sight of God and all the people, and how the chief priests and our rulers delivered Him to the sentence of death, and crucified Him. But we were hoping that it was He who was going to redeem Israel. Indeed, besides all this, it is the

third day since these things happened. But also some women among us amazed us. When they were at the tomb early in the morning, and did not find His body, they came, saying that they had also seen a vision of angels who said that He was alive. Some of those who were with us went to the tomb and found it just exactly as the women also had said; but Him they did not see." And He said to them, "O foolish men and slow of heart to believe in all that the prophets have spoken! Was it not necessary for the Christ to suffer these things and to enter into His glory?" Then beginning with Moses and with all the prophets, He explained to them the things concerning Himself in all the Scriptures. And they approached the village where they were going, and He acted as though He were going farther. But they urged Him, saying, "Stay with us, for it is getting toward evening, and the day is now nearly over." So He went in to stay with them. When He had reclined at the table with them, He took the bread and blessed it, and breaking it, He began giving it to them. Then their eyes were opened and they recognized Him; and He vanished from their sight. They said to one another, "Were not our hearts burning within us while He was speaking to us on the road, while He was explaining the Scriptures to us?" And they got up that very hour and returned to Jerusalem, and found gathered together the eleven and those who were with them, saying, "The Lord has really risen and has appeared to Simon." They began to relate their experiences on the road and how He was recognized by them in the breaking of the bread. While they were telling these things, He Himself stood in their midst and said to them, "Peace be to you." But they were startled and frightened and thought that they were seeing a spirit. And He said to them, "Why are you troubled, and why do doubts arise in your hearts? See My hands and My feet, that it is I Myself; touch Me and see, for a spirit does not have flesh and bones as you see that I have." And when He had said this, He showed them His hands and His feet. While they still could not believe it because of their joy and amazement, He said to them, "Have you anything here to eat?" They gave Him a piece of a broiled fish; and He took it and ate it before them. Now He said to them, "These are My words which I spoke to you while I was still with you, that all things which are written about Me in the Law of Moses and the Prophets and the Psalms must be fulfilled." Then He opened their minds to understand the Scriptures, and He said to them, "Thus it is written, that the Christ would suffer and rise again from the dead the third day, and that repentance for forgiveness of sins would be proclaimed in His name to all the nations, beginning from Jerusalem. You are witnesses of these things. And behold, I am sending forth the promise of My Father upon you; but you are to stay in the city until you are clothed with power from on high." And He led them out as far as Bethany, and He lifted up His hands and blessed them. While He was blessing them, He parted from them and was carried up into heaven. And they, after worshiping Him, returned to Jerusalem with great joy, and were continually in the temple praising God.

Comment: Gautama Siddhartha died, and there is no account of his resurrection from the dead. Nor was there any prophecy of his birth. Whereas the continual prophesies of the coming saviour of mankind from about 3500 BC by many prophets of old all came to fulfilment. This is definitely a must for all to consider—a *great Saviour* for their time on this earth! *What a tremendous shame if you do not, as it will affect you for eternity!* You will read the tremendous authority and power over all things, unlike anyone else on this earth, witnessed by his disciples and many others. That is impossible to dismiss as just fairy tales or hearsays. You are faced by the factual evidences, as compared to the teachings of Buddha or Gautama Siddhartha, and need to come to your own conclusion.

18

Gautama Siddhartha's Path of Enlightenment (*Self-Realization)

A. Buddha's Four Noble Truths

The Four Noble Truths is the foundational anchor for the basis of Buddhism, and it is made up of the (i) Dukkha, (ii) Samudaya, (iii) Nirodha, and (iv) Magga, and only those who had attained Buddhahood or Nirvana, which is the same is the *Self-Realization in Vedic Hinduism, are capable of understanding or comprehending the truths or realities. So the truths or realities is Dukkha, the rising of the Dukkha (Samudaya), cessation of the Dukkha (Nirodha), and the path leading to the cessation of the Dukkha (Magga). The Four Noble Truths are Buddha's interpretations of Hinduism's the path of freedom from attachments or the renunciation of all attachments, and that is also called self-realization, in order to achieve the Atman or being one with the god, Brahman, Vishnu, or Krishna. In other words, the Four Noble Truth is a path to be one "as or equal with god."

(i) *Dukkha* is the craving and clinging to the impermanent states and things, which is incapable of satisfying and painful.

(ii) *Samudaya* is the source or the rising of the Dukkha. The continuing thirst, craving, and hunger for the impermanent states and things resulted in the continuing reincarnation of life in this world, trapped in rebirths, and renewed dissatisfaction, and therefore the inability to escape from these continual rebirths into the world (i.e., getting stuck in the Samsara cycle).

(iii) *Nirodha* is the cessation of the Dukkha by stopping this craving and attachment, thus arriving at Buddhahood or Nirvana, and therefore escaping from the continuous rebirths and dissatisfaction and attachment to things.

(iv) *Magga* is the path to the cessation of or liberation from the Dukkha by following the Noble Eightfold Path, which provides a way of restraining and disciplining oneself through the practice of mindful meditation resulting in the cessation of craving, thirst, and clinging, therefore ending the continuous rebirths and dissatisfaction.

B. Buddha's Golden Rule: The Noble Eightfold Path

The *Noble Eightfold Path* is man's way of achieving *perfect happiness* without relying or submitting to a god or any god. The result is a total eradication of negative feelings like anger, hatred, fear, worry, restlessness, and the cessation of cravings, lusts, greed, and covetousness for power and control. This is attained by sheer mental power and resolve of the person through hours of meditation and chanting that can go on for years until *perfection* is reached. It is essentially reaching a state of no feeling and becoming mindless or thoughtless, and therefore reaching a state of Nirvana. For the Western readers, it is actually the ultimate goal or utopia of Abraham Maslow's theory of *self-actualization. In following a path, one step follows the other, and therefore there is a need or necessity for the follower to have an understanding or comprehension of each step before taking on the other.* How much a follower needs to understand is a nonquantifiable measure, and that is left to the student and or the leading teacher and or leading Buddhist monk.

Here are the Noble Eightfold Path (Words are from Sanskrit): *Panna (Wisdom):*

(i)   *Perfect understanding* or *vision* (Samma Ditthi) of what the *I* or ego is, and what are the reality of all our desperate lusts and covetousness for those animate and inanimate objects that failed to satisfy us in this life.

(ii)   *Perfect thought* and *intention* or *aspiration* (Samma Sankappa) to guide and direct one's life, and that means having the *right perspective,* and acting from love and compassion, and being free to practice letting go. *Sila (Discipline):*

(iii) *Perfect speech* (Samma-Vaca). This is also called the right speech, which is clear, truthful, uplifting, and nonharmful communication.

(iv)   *Perfect action* (Samma Kammanta). This is also called right action where the ethical foundation of life is based on the principle of nonexploitation of oneself or others.

(v)   *Perfect livelihood* (Samma Ajiva). The right livelihood that is based on the ethical principle of nonexploitation, which is the basis of a utopian society. *Samadhi (Mental state of quietness like in a trance)*

(vi)   *Perfect effort* (Samma Vayama). Full or complete effort and vitality of consciously directing life's energy toward the transformative path of creative and healing actions that engenders wholeness.

(vii) *Perfect mindfulness* (Samma Sati). Perfect awareness or right mindfulness of things, oneself, people, feelings, thoughts, and reality.

(viii) *Perfect concentration* (Samma Samadhi). Purifying of the whole mind through fixed, total absorption of concentration and meditation to a single-mindedness of the thought.

Comments: After going through the Four Noble Truths and the Noble Eightfold Path, one cannot help but be impressed by the

severity and complete commitment that is required in order to follow the way of the Buddha (Gautama Siddhartha) that there can be
no less than abandoning all and spend a lifetime of meditation to
achieve Nirvana or of becoming a Bodhisattva, knowing that there
is no evidence of Nirvana at all or the existence of a Bodhisattva.
It is definitely not everyone's cup of tea but only for the very few.
The Noble Eightfold Path is nothing but a further expansion of the
Four Noble Truths. Different sects of Buddhism use the Four Noble
Truths and Eightfold Paths as a base and expanded them to suit their
own interpretations on how to achieve Nirvana. Therefore, it is a
religion where only the very few can achieve *perfection* or Nirvana,
and the remainder will spend countless number of lifetimes stuck in
the *Samsara cycle. Whereas in Christianity, a person is accepted into
the kingdom of heaven and inherits eternal life the second a person
repents and confesses that Jesus Christ is the Begotten Son of God
who gave His life for the sinner and was resurrected from the dead.

Non-Self (Anatta-Pali or Anatman-Sanskrit)

Non-self is one of the foundational doctrine in Buddhism. It
essentially describes a person as non-self—without soul and non-es-
sence—and is therefore changing continuously. It is one of the three
key pillars of Buddhism, and the other two are Anicca (impermanence, nothing lasts) and Dukkha (suffering, unsatisfactory innate
birth, aging, death, rebirth and redeath which is the Samsara cycle).
Even as Anatta is a basic doctrine, it is not without controversy
among various Buddhist sects.

C. Sangha (Community)

The Sangha was founded by Gautama Siddhartha and is made
up of monks (Bhikkhus) and nuns (Bhikkhuni), whose aim is to turn
away from the concerns of a materialistic world and to concentrate
on the development through intense study, meditation, and physical
discipline. They are not to worry where the next meal comes from.
The intent is that the monks and nuns provide guidance and support

to the general Buddhist population, who in turn will provide meals to the monks and nuns. The monks and nuns regard themselves as people who had been reborn but at different stages of the Samsara cycle, and therefore at a higher level to the general population. It is an interesting relationship whereby those who are superior or at a higher level depend on the inferior or lower level for their daily sustenance. It is almost parasitic in relationship. That symbiotic relationship extends to more than just food but also clothes, means of travel, medicine, shelter, etc.

All members of the sangha observe a set of strict monastery rules known as Vinaya in order to help the aspirants achieve their individual goals. Anyone is free to leave the order at any time.

It does seem that the sangha is equivalent to the Roman Catholic monastery.

D. Buddhist Good and Bad Works

Buddhism, like Islam and many other religions, believes in doing good works or acts of generosity, which they earn merits toward their final end or give them karmic rewards. In Buddhism, there are many kinds of merits, and some are worth more than the other. The development and advancement of the recipient also determines the degrees of merit accrued. Does one so-called bad deed cancel out one good work or several good works no one knows, as it is all up in the air or in the Samsara cycle? How does the Samsara cycle keep track of the good and bad deeds of everyone on this earth and every living organism? Furthermore, what it means is that every time a Buddhist does a good deed, it is always with an ulterior motive for him or her to move up the Samsara cycle. It is called the *virtues of selfishness*. So in reality, it is a religion of selfish people who are always thinking about themselves first and foremost in all that they do. Will fifty good deeds cancel out a murder or a lie? It does seem that this type of argument is left unresolved, and Buddhists elect to allow and surrender their karma or fate of their life after death to be determined by the brainless, mindless nonentity called the Samsara cycle.

The difficulty with *good works* is that a rich person is capable of doing more good works and therefore able to get off the Samsara cycle much earlier than most ordinary person on the street. Or an able person is more capable of doing good works than a disabled person, or does the Samsara cycle take that into consideration? Therefore, it is an inescapable conclusion that the present status of any person on earth today is because of what he or she was in their past life! Then the argument that can be made is why help them now because they do deserve their fate or karma? Why help someone who is probably a serial killer in his or her past life? So for a Buddhist, good works come from selfishness.

The Buddhist ideology is very self-serving to the monk and nuns because they provide you a chance and opportunity for the layperson to do good works, and therefore, elevate their status in the Samsara cycle. The monks and nuns go out once a day, and with other branch of Buddhism, twice a day, begging for their daily sustenance and there provides you an opportunity or chance for good works. Whereas they themselves do nothing but chant and meditate so that they can achieve a higher status in the Samsara cycle! It is nothing short of a parasitic, symbiotic relationship.

Buddhism does not produce any documented lists of *bad works* that result in demerits. Who and what then decides what are demerits? If a jury in the court of law decided that the person on trial for murder is guilty and the judge handed out a judgment of death by lethal injection, is that a demerit or a merit for the judge who made the decision? How about the members of the jury? Everything is left in the air for the Samsara cycle to decide, and everyone who died will be reborn in the appropriate level in the Samsara cycle. The Samsara cycle is both judge and jury and had become an inanimate *ethereal god* that makes all the decisions with tremendous power over and knowledge of all the good and bad that everyone had done, including all living things, as they are part of the Samsara cycle. Once the concept of the Samsara cycle falls apart, there goes Buddhism also.

Buddhism does not deal with the root cause of the cravings, lust, greed, desires, etc. but puts up a noble fight through willpower and meditation to suppress against all of it. To suppress it means that it continues to lay hidden away, and it does not mean its eradication or that a person had conquered it all. The long periods of not appearing does not mean it is not there.

19

Christian Doctrines on Good Works and Dead Works

Matthew 5:38–48 (~AD 30–60) says,

> You have heard that it was said, *"An eye for an eye, and a tooth for a tooth."* But I say to you, do not resist an evil person; but whoever slaps you on your right cheek, turn the other to him also. If anyone wants to sue you and take your shirt, let him have your coat also. Whoever forces you to go one mile, go with him two. Give to him who asks of you, and do not turn away from him who wants to borrow from you. You have heard that it was said, *"You shall love your neighbor* and hate your enemy." But I say to you, love your enemies and pray for those who persecute you, so that you may be sons of your Father who is in heaven; for He causes His sun to rise on the evil and the good, and sends rain on the righteous and the unrighteous. For if you love those who love you, what reward do you have? Do not even the tax collectors do the same? If you greet only your brothers, what more are you doing than others?

Do not even the Gentiles do the same? Therefore you are to be perfect, as your heavenly Father is perfect.

James 2:13–26 (~AD 62) says,

> For judgment will be merciless to one who has shown no mercy; mercy triumphs over judgment. What use is it, my brethren, if someone says he has faith but he has no works? Can that faith save him? If a brother or sister is without clothing and in need of daily food, and one of you says to them, "Go in peace, be warmed and be filled," and yet you do not give them what is necessary for their body, what use is that? Even so faith, if it has no works, is dead, being by itself. But someone may well say, "You have faith and I have works; show me your faith without the works, and I will show you my faith by my works." You believe that God is one. You do well; the demons also believe, and shudder. But are you willing to recognize, you foolish fellow, that faith without works is useless? Was not Abraham our father justified by works when he offered up Isaac his son on the altar? You see that faith was working with his works, and as a result of the works, faith was perfected; and the Scripture was fulfilled which says, "*And Abraham believed god, and it was reckoned to him as righteousness,*" and he was called the friend of God. You see that a man is justified by works and not by faith alone. In the same way, was not Rahab, the harlot, also justified by works when she received the messengers and sent them out by another way? For just as the body without the spirit is dead, so also faith without works is dead.

Hebrews 6:1–2 (~AD 64) says, "Therefore leaving the elementary teaching about the Christ, let us press on to maturity, not laying again a foundation of *repentance from dead works* and of faith toward God, of instruction about washings and laying on of hands, and the resurrection of the dead and eternal judgment."

Hebrews 9:13–14 says, "For if the blood of goats and bulls and the ashes of a heifer sprinkling those who have been defiled sanctify for the cleansing of the flesh, how much more will the blood of Christ, who through the eternal Spirit offered Himself without blemish to God, *cleanse your conscience from dead works* to serve the living God?"

Clarification

In Christianity, good works are a result of *faith* in God the Father and in His Begotten Son who gave His life on the cross that all may be saved from eternal damnation. Out of faith is the *love of God*, and it is the sharing of the love of God to all, friend or foe, in terms of words or deeds to all the very mark of a Christian. So the essence of Christianity is the love of God to all our neighbours, friends, or foes. Good works are things that are done as a result of faith, as well as doing those things according to the will of God. So it stands to reason that dead works are the result of the soul, will, and of the flesh. Even those things that are done in the name of God and for God can be dead works because they did not come from God. The works can have a dressing or appearance of grandeur and magnificence and still be dead works from God's perspective. Unless it is done in God's way, He will have no part of it. In His word in Isaiah 42:8, "I am the Lord, that is My name, and My Glory I will not give another."

There were two James in the New Testament of the Bible. One is James the brother of John, both of whom were sons of Zebedee. The other James is the earthly brother of Jesus. Jesus, the Son of God, was the son of Mary who was impregnated by the Holy Spirit, and therefore did not have an earth father. James was the son of Mary and a carpenter by the name of Joseph, therefore James was the half-brother of Jesus who grew up with Jesus. James was an elder in the

Church in Jerusalem in around AD 62. James was thrown from the roof of the temple, then beaten and clubbed to death. It is of tremendous testimony that James, the half-brother of Jesus who grew up with him and witnessed at firsthand Jesus's humanity, sharing the same mother, admitted and confessed Jesus as the Begotten Son of God who gave His life on the cross for the sins of humanity!

In Christianity, a person cannot gain salvation and obtain eternal life through good works as shown in Ephesian 2:8–9, "For by grace you have been saved through faith; and that not of yourselves, it is the gift of God not as a result of works, so that no one may boast." This is contrary to the concept of the Samsara cycle where a person can achieve a higher level in the Samsara cycle by earning lots of merits!

20

Buddhist Spiritists

SPIRITISTS OR MEDIUMS IN BUDDHISM

Some sects of Buddhism, like Tibetan Buddhism and in Taoism, do practice divination, astral travel, acted as mediums, and well as spiritists. Most of the Buddhist temples in Southeast Asia are dedicated to their revered ascended immortals or deities. All these practices are forbidden by God according to the scriptures in Bible, as quoted below. Also, Christians are forbidden from calling up the dead, as that is what a spiritist does. **What that means is, the minute you start talking to, praying to or for the dead, then you are calling on the dead.** In some Christian cult or sect, they do pray and talk to some of their dead like the "virgin Mary," saint Christopher, saint Jude, etc., which is forbidden according to the scriptures in the Old testament of the Bible as well as in the Gospel of Matthew 8:22 where Jesus said, "Follow Me and Let the dead bury the dead." And what He is saying in essence is do not bother the dead at all.

CHRISTIAN DOCTRINES ON SPIRITISTS AND MEDIUMS

Leviticus 20:26–27: "Thus you are to be holy to Me, for I the LORD am holy; and I have set you apart from the peoples to be Mine. 'Now a man or a woman, who is a **medium or a spiritist,** shall surely be put to death. They shall be stoned with stones, their blood guiltiness is upon them.'"

Deut. 18:10–12: "There shall not be found among you anyone who makes his son or his daughter pass through the fire, one who uses **divination**, one who practices **witchcraft**, or one who interprets omens, or a **sorcerer**, or one who casts a spell, or a **medium**, or a **spiritist**, or **one who calls up the dead.** For whoever does these things is detestable to the LORD; and because of these detestable things the LORD your God will drive them out before you."

2 Chron 33:6: "He made his sons pass through the fire in the valley of Ben-Hinnom; and he practiced **witchcraft**, used divination, practiced sorcery and dealt with **mediums** and **spiritists**. He did much evil in the sight of the LORD, provoking Him to anger."

21

Buddhist *Meditation

A. General

Volumes had been written on the different Buddhist meditation methods, and they vary depending on the different schools of Buddhism. It is not the intent of this writing to expound on the various Buddhist meditation methods but only to capture the essence of it and compare it to meditation practices according to biblical scriptures. Meditation is a major part of the life of Buddhist monks and nuns and some Buddhist believers, as it is the key and foundational practice to suppressing all the cravings, lust, desires, greed, and wants. Buddhist pursues meditation as part of the path or route toward Nirvana or being enlightened. The different techniques are aimed to develop mindfulness, concentration, extra powers, tranquility, and insight, and also to remove unwholesome qualities that are an impediment to liberation, such as kindness to remove ill will, hate, anger, and cravings. In the Theravada tradition alone, there are some fifty methods for developing mindfulness and forty for developing concentration. In the Tibetan tradition, there are thousands for visualization meditations.

Many Buddhist teachings require that the person have the right posture, though not a must, eyes closed to avoid distractions, and focusing and visualizing sometimes on the statue or image of the Buddha, and at the same time practicing their breathing techniques, and most importantly, relaxation. All the while, the meditator has to guard against cravings, desires, waves of drowsiness, and lethargy, etc. and if distracted, one is to start over again to refocus to empty one's mind and thoughts. As long as nothing comes into the mind, it is regarded as being stable, calm, and serene. Once that is achieved, the meditator can begin to explore the nature of his or her consciousness and mind. It does take a lot of short practices, like fifteen to twenty minutes each day and possibly several times a day. Thought itself is an object of awareness without distractions, and it will fade out of the meditator's consciousness, and what remains between the vanishing of one thought and the rising of another is awareness, emptiness, and without obstruction, like empty spaces or blankness. The Buddhist teaching is that *by releasing the tension that binds the mind*, the meditator undoubtedly brings about inner freedom. Patience and persisting the practice makes perfect. For the Buddhist, the meditation eventually becomes effortless, and then he or she can sustain each session for hours on end.

In the Pali Canon, the Buddha regarded Samatha (serenity or tranquility which steadies, composes, unifies, and concentrates the mind) and Vipassana (insight which enables one to explore and discern) meditation practices as the two qualities of the mind to be developed through meditation.

B. Chanting *Mantra (Prayer)

Mantra is a sequence of words or syllables that are chanted, usually repetitively, as part of a Buddhist practice. Again, this is very similar to Vedic Hindu mantram as can be found in chapter 35. Buddhism came up with their own version, but the root and intent are the same.

Other branches of Buddhism use repetitive chanting of a mantra as a form of meditation. This practice of calling the Buddha to mind by repeating his name is to bring all his focus upon the Buddha. This can be done vocally or mentally, with or without the use of prayer beads.

Chanting mantra is another way of bringing the mind to a singleness of focus. It is also another borrowed technique from Hinduism and the ascetic Yogis. It numbs the mind and thought to take or strip away any kind of distraction and cravings or desires in order to bring the mind to a state of constant rest with nothingness. The chanting can go on and on for hours.

C. Examples of Different Buddhist Mantras:

i.   Avalokitesvara Mantra: "Om Mani Padme Hum."

Om is a sacred syllable and sound in Hinduism and is adopted into Buddhism and other religions. *Mani* means jewel or bead, *padme* is the lotus flower, and *hum* represents the spirit of enlightenment. The symbol of om has deep spiritual meaning in all Hindu dharmas, but the meanings and connotations vary among the different schools and sects. In Hinduism, it refers to the Atman (soul, self within) and Brahman (ultimate reality, the universe, truth, divine, supreme spirit, cosmic principles, knowledge). For the sect of Buddhism that has no God in its belief, then the meaning of the word om has a more altruistic perspective and leans toward that of ultimate reality, cosmic principles, wisdom, and knowledge.

With the development of Buddhism over the years, this mantra with its six syllables took on added meaning, such as a representation of the purification of the six realms of existence. For example:

- *Om* with generosity purifies pride/ego;
- *Ma* with ethics purifies jealousy/lusts;
- *Ni* with patience purifies passion/desire;
- *Pad* with diligence purifies ignorance/prejudice;
- *Me* with renunciation purifies greed/possessiveness; and
- *Hum* with wisdom purifies aggression/hatred.

Buddhists believe that it invokes powerful benevolent attention and blessing with the embodiment of compassion.

ii. Shakyamuni Mantra: "Om Muni Mahamuni Shakyamuni Svaha."

Shakyamuni (Gautama Buddha of the clan of Shakyan): "Om wise one, wise one, great wise one to the wise one of the Shakyanshail."

iii. Amitabaha Mantra: "Om Amideva Hrij."

It is recited to overcome obstacles and hindrances in that it protects the believer from all hindrances to success.

iv. White (Sita) Tara Mantra: "Om Tare Tuttare Ture Mama Ayuh Punya Jnana Pustim Kuru Svaha."

White Tara is associated to long life, and she is pictured as being endowed with seven eyes (eye on the palm of her hands, soles of her feet, and forehead) to symbolize the watchfulness of the compassionate mind.

v. Green Tara Mantra: "Om Tare Tuttare Ture Soha."

The Green Tara Mantra is used to overcome physical, mental, and emotional blockages in relationship. The believer is to release his or her hanging on to a particular outcome or result because it is self-defeating and creates unhappiness and agitations.

vi. Medicine Buddha Mantra: "Tayata Om Bekanze Maha Bekanze Radza Samudgate Soha."

Its mantra is recited for success, and it is supposed to help eliminate problems, unhappiness, and suffering. Some Buddhists believe that if recited at time of near death, the person will not be rebirthed into this life of suffering and pain but will enter what it called *pure land.* Some believe that the mantra can also affect animals! Pure land is a place where certain Buddhist groups or schools believe is a place to escape to instead of being stuck in the Samsara cycle, but really has no clear definition, location, or details of what pure land is.

vii. Vajrapani Mantra: "Om Vajrapani Hum."

Vajrapani is a Bodhisattva, a person who had attained Nirvana but refused to cross over and stayed behind to help others on earth, and he represents the energy of an enlightened mind and is pictured dancing wildly within a halo of flame, which represents transformation. He holds a thunderbolt (vajra) in his right hand, which emphasizes the power to cut through the darkness of delusion, and he is completely free from hatred.

Comments: It is interesting to note that Buddhists believe that when chanting a mantra, it can change a person or events. To put it simply, it is akin to saying that if you say it sufficiently, you become what you say. For example, if you empty your mind of pride and focus on a deity and continuously chant "I am humble," that eventually, you are humble. It is a false supposition and a fallacy. A person may feel that he or she had defeated or conquered pride for a while, but it will rear its ugly head when the occasion presents itself. Just because we do not feel it does not mean it is not there, as it is present in its latent form.

One of the goals of a Buddhist is to defeat suffering and pain in life, but suffering and pain is the taskmaster and the anvil of life to bring a man to his knees and learn humility. Just to behave humbly gives an appearance of being humble and does not necessarily mean a person is humble. Furthermore, the irony is to give an appearance of humility is actually pride in disguise. True humility does not come naturally, even as it is pure in its essence. The Bible says that all men sinned and short of the glory of God. So all men have the root of sin, and no matter how hard mankind exercise the different techniques to get rid of it, it does not mean it is ridden off. In the practice of Buddhism, all that happens in meditation is the suppression of it (cravings, lusts, greed, desires, want, etc.), and that does not get rid of the root of *sin* in men. Suppression means that it is pushed back and not the erasing of it. So in reality, if a Buddhist can only suppress sin, he or she will be stuck in the Samsara cycle forever and will never escape hell on earth.

To think that anyone can attain the purity of no sin is self-deception of the highest order. There is a major difference between suppressing sin and conquering sin. The wage of sin is death. A Buddhist tries to suppress sin, but Jesus Christ conquered sin and death by the evidence of His death and resurrection! The sting of death is sin, and the power of sin is the law. In the Bible, God had given the Ten Commandments, as well as some 660 ordinances and statutes, and it is impossible to keep all that and is therefore referred to as a curse. And the curse was removed by the crucifixion of Jesus Christ on the cross (tree).

According to biblical scriptures, when lust is conceived, it gives birth to sin, and when sin is accomplished, it brings forth death. But for those who believe in the work of Jesus Christ, the begotten Son of God, on the cross and His resurrection, the Spirit of life on Jesus Christ is what sets the believers free from the law of sin and death. *Only God can save mankind, as mankind is incapable of saving himself, unless mankind is too proud to accept God's gift and feels that he or she is more than capable and strong enough to save him or herself!*

It is very important to know that the original intent and purpose of Buddhist meditation and mantra comes from the ancient Vedic Hindu texts as referred to in chapter 35. Firstly, your yogic pose during meditation is that of a serpentine pose where the spinal column is upright and the energy comes from the base of the serpentine coil. Furthermore, the meditation and mantra is to destroy the person's willpower so that a foreign entity or spirit can enter the person through the sagittal aperture. This is a very serious matter as it is spiritual possession by a foreign entity. You can read all that in the Ancient Sacred Vedic Hindu Text References in chapter 35. It may seem like a small matter, but the consequences are horrendous, and you can be possessed without your knowledge. Little knowledge is a dangerous thing. There is right and wrong meditation. Christian meditation is very much different according to the scriptures.

22

Christian Meditation
(To Contemplate or To Reflect)

Psalms 19:14 (~1035–961 BC) says, "Let the words of my mouth and *the meditation of my heart* Be acceptable in Your sight, O Lord, my rock and my Redeemer."

Psalms 49:3 says, "My mouth will speak wisdom, And the meditation of my heart will be understanding."

Psalms 104:33–34 says, "I will sing to the LORD as long as I live; I will sing praise to my God while I have my being. *Let my meditation be pleasing to Him;* As for me, I shall be glad in the Lord."

Psalms 119:97–107 says,

> Mem. O how I love Your law! It is my meditation all the day. Your commandments make me wiser than my enemies, For they are ever mine. I have more insight than all my teachers, For Your testimonies are my meditation. I understand more than the aged, because I have observed Your precepts. I have restrained my feet from every evil way, That I may keep Your word. I have not turned aside from Your ordinances, For You Yourself have taught me. How sweet are Your words to my taste! Yes, sweeter than honey

to my mouth! From Your precepts I get under-standing; Therefore I hate every false way. Nun. Your word is a lamp to my feet And a light to my path. I have sworn and I will confirm it, That I will keep Your righteous ordinances. I am exceed-ingly afflicted; Revive me, O Lord, according to Your word.

Psalms 143:5–6 says, "I remember the days of old; *I meditate on all Your doings;* I muse on the work of Your hands. I stretch out my hands to You; My soul longs for You, as a parched land. Selah."

Psalms 145:5–9 says,

I will extol You, my God, O King, And I will bless Your name forever and ever. Every day I will bless You, And I will praise Your name forever and ever. Great is the Lord, and highly to be praised, And His greatness is unsearch-able. One generation shall praise Your works to another, And shall declare Your mighty acts. On the glorious splendour of Your majesty *And on Your wonderful works, I will meditate.* Men shall speak of the power of Your awesome acts, And I will tell of Your greatness. They shall eagerly utter the memory of Your abundant goodness And will shout joyfully of Your righteousness. The Lord is gracious and merciful; Slow to anger and great in loving kindness. The Lord is good to all, And His mercies are over all His works.

Matthew 6:5–8 (~AD 30–64) says,

"When you pray, you are not to be like the hypocrites; for they love to stand and pray in the synagogues and on the street corners so that they may be seen by men. Truly I say to you, they have their reward in full. But you, when you pray, go into your inner room, close your door and pray to your Father who is in secret, and your Father who sees what is done in secret will reward you. *And when you are praying, do not use meaningless repetition as the Gentiles do, for they suppose that they will be heard for their many words." So do not be like them; for your Father knows what you need before you ask Him.*

Philippians 4:8–9 (~AD 49–51) says, "Finally, brethren, whatever is true, whatever is honourable, whatever is right, whatever is pure, whatever is lovely, whatever is of good repute, if there is any excellence and if anything worthy of praise, *dwell on these things.* The things you have learned and received and heard and seen in me, practice these things, and the God of peace will be with you."

Comments: Meditation by the followers of Christ is very different from that of Buddhist meditation in several ways. For the believers of Christ, meditation comes from the heart for the love of God and His Begotten Son because God the Father had sacrificed His Son for sin so that the believers are saved from the judgment of sin, attain eternal life, and live to serve and worship God. What the believers of Christ do is focus on the Word of God, Who He is, and His deeds. What happens here is phenomenal in that the Holy Spirit of God will quicken the believers with the revelation of the wisdom and mystery of His Word, and they are enlightened and transformed by that revelation. The believers are sometimes filled with joy and sometimes are awed at the wonderment of God's love toward him or her during meditation. This is the fellowship of God and His faithful believers when the holy, eternal, and almighty touches them who are mortal, base, foolish, and temporary. It is a joyous thing to meditate on God and His word, which is very contrary to that of a Buddhist's meditation to suppress all his cravings, lusts, desires, wants, and needs, etc.

23a.

Veneration

To venerate someone is to place high respect or honour to that someone, and that comes in how the respect is shown. Respect is normally shown in how we address, speak about, or speak to the person that one is venerating. When meeting with a king, queen, or even a high official, people sometimes bring gifts to show that respect and high regard. So the subject would bow or do a curtsey to their king or queen as a form of respect or veneration. However, when the same is done for someone who is dead and buried, it takes on a different perspective.

In many Buddhist homes, especially those that practice Taoism, there are pictures of parents and grandparents hanging on the wall, and oftentimes there is an incense pot with burning incense sticks in it and sometimes a bowl of fruits offerings beside the pot. There is really nothing wrong to have pictures of relatives or parents hanging on the wall, but it is what a person does with the pictures. The dead is dead, as they do not eat, drink, speak, talk, see, or listen to what is said or being done! It is like a rock on the roadside. Therefore, the incense pot, burning incense sticks, and bowl of fruits are more for the living than the dead.

From the person who executes such practices, they can be for several reasons, and these are as follows:

(i)   That they can affect the status of the dead.

        If the living can affect the status of the dead by words of prayer and offerings, then it is possible to save Adolf Hitler (Germany), Stalin (Russia), and General Pol Pot (Cambodia), who authorized the killing of millions, from judgment and eternal damnation! The same argument can be applied to Adolf Hitler, Stalin, and General Pol Pot in that they can save themselves by doing good works worthy of merit points when they entered into the Samsara cycle and eventually save themselves and achieve Nirvana. It is just too bad for those who suffered and died at the hands of the killers. Those innocent lives will have to work out their own salvation when they enter into the Samsara cycle. What this really means in the Buddhist's perspective is that you can always save yourself regardless of what hideous acts you had committed because once you enter into the Samsara cycle, you can always do good works and come out smelling like a rose, coming back in the afterlife, and be prosperous and living a luxurious life. So, logically, it is difficult to see how this practice stands up in a common-sense perspective. Similarly, the largest Christian sect or cult, Roman Catholicism, also practice prayers for the dead in hope of putting the status of the dead in a better position, which is a heresy, according to the Bible. This is differentiated from individual Catholic believers in that they may not concur with such practices.

        Further, the Taoist Buddhists practice the burning for such items, like papier-mâché houses, cars, computer laptops, and paper *money rolls* to represent money for their beloved dead relatives and continues to thrive in many Asian societies. But then, the dead do not eat, drink, speak, talk, walk, or run; therefore, the practice is nothing but vanity. When I interviewed the representatives of a

Buddhists' association that encourages such practices, they agreed that they are making millions of dollars for their enterprise. What speaks volumes is what are not burnt as sacrifices to the dead, which are toilet paper, under shorts, or a change of clothes, which are a must because if they do eat and drink, they definitely have those items.

(ii) That they can talk with or pray to the dead to intercede in their lives.

The minute a person talks with or prays to the dead for favours or to intercede, it presupposes that the dead has certain authority and power to affect the lives of the living, and that power crosses the line between the dead and the living. It is a very thin line between veneration and idolatry. And I believe that thin line is crossed when that happened, that is, talking with or praying to the dead. Not only Buddhists do it, but the largest Christian cult or sect, Roman Catholicism, also does it. Roman Catholicism has their Saint Christopher, Saint Jude, the Virgin Mary, etc. Of course, Roman Catholicism also make millions of dollars selling indulgences. The Roman Catholics have elevated the status of some of the dead to that of ascended immortals or deities, much like that of Buddhism where the dead have the authority and power to cross over and affect the lives of the living. This practice of paganism predates Christianity by more than a thousand years, and it can be found in Egypt, Rome, Middle East, and Africa. Sometimes it is called parentalia, the worship of parents and the worship of the dead, and it crosses the line between putting a memory of someone in high regard versus talking, praying, and communicating with the dead.

Both Taoist and Tibetan Buddhism have pantheon of deities who are ascended immortals that cover all the different jurisdictions of the heavens and earth and the needs of mankind.

Many of the Buddhists and practicing Roman Catholic believers talk and pray to the dead directly, and others talk to the dead through mediums. This is forbidden according to the Christian Holy Bible. According to the scriptures, *Leviticus 19:31 (~1445 BC)* says, "Do not turn to mediums or spiritualists; do not seek them out to be defiled by them. I am the LORD your God," and *Leviticus 20:6* says, "As for the person who turns to mediums and to spiritualists, to play the harlot after them, I will also set My face against that person and will cut him off from among his people."

In Taoism, the Jade Emperor is regarded as the highest deity, ascended immortal, and it is sometimes considered as the Three Pure Ones, which is made up of the Jade Emperor (Yuhuang), Great Jade Emperor (Yuhuang Dadi), and Supreme Jade Emperor (Yuhuang Shangdi). The Jade Emperor is the supreme leader of the heavens, hell, and is the protector of all mankind. There are hundreds of deities that it is impossible to put them all down on paper in a meaningful way. So I am going to just list some of the interesting main deities:

- Avalokitesvara (The one who regards the world sounds, Kuan Shih Yin Pu Sa). The protector from eight fears (fire, wind or storm, attack from snakes, tigers, bandits, elephant or captivity, evil spirits or demons, drowning, and falling off a cliff);
- Jiang Tai Gong;
- Queen of Heaven (Tian Hu Sheng Mu);
- The Supreme Lord of the Dark Heaven (Xuan Tian Shang Ti);
- Imperial Wen Chang (Wen Chang Di Jun);
- The Door God (Men Shen);
- The Mysterious Lady of the Ninth Heaven (Jiu Tian Xuan Nu);
- The Great Spirits of the Earth (Fu De Zheng Shen);
- The Thunder God (Lei Gong); and
- The Kitchen God (Zao Jun, Zao Shen or Zhange Lang).

The Eight Immortals

(iii) That they do it out of guilt because of what they did not do while their parents were alive, or that they do purely out of remembrance and respect.

Confucius (551–479 BC) made a significant impact on the Asian life and mind-set, as he championed strong family loyalty, ancestor veneration, respect of elders by their children, and of husband by wives. So deep was the impact on people's lives that it was incorporated into the practice of the Buddhist Taoist religion. And this is where it crossed the line between honour and veneration versus worship. It was never Confucius's intent for the people to worship their elders and ancestors but to honour and respect them. Then it progressed into a great way of making money for the temples by the sale of food, incense, *rolled-up paper* to represent money, and papier-mâché houses, cars, etc., by the burning of them for the offering to the dead. So what started as an honourable thing to do became a practice and ritual of worship, and the line became dulled, blurred, and is a travesty. This practice and ritual is passed on through many generations, and many of today's generation just assume the practice and that it is just a ritual of honour and respect. And they do not even question it or even realize that they have crossed the line and that it had become idol worship!

23b

What Is an Idol or Buddhist Deity?

The minute a person assumes that the inanimate object or a dead person that is not God has the power and authority to answer prayers or requests, then it crossed the line between the dead and the living. It can be talking to or praying to or make offerings to someone that is dead, or animal or an inanimate object. An idol is like a rock or a carving, a picture, a statue that cannot and is unable to respond or communicate with the worshipper. A deity in the Buddhist sense is a dead person who was exceptional in his works and deeds while on earth and is now revered, highly honoured, worshipped, and is regarded as an ascended immortal. The only time it is able to communicate back is when it is from demons and evil spirits. Buddhism, even Theravada Buddhism, admits that there are evil spirits and demons but is unable to clearly define who and what they are.

With that many deities, there are so many questions regarding how they work together and how they do resolve disagreements regarding power, authority, and who assigned them their power, authority, and daily tasks, etc. If they are previously mortals, surely those conflicts will certainly arise, and who says they do not? However, clever Buddhists and *man* have assigned them responsibilities so that there is peace in the heavenly realms. Is there a war in the realm of the ascended immortals over jurisdiction, authority, and power, etc.?

In the history of Indian Hinduism, there are battles among the hundreds of deities in the heavens with chariots and flying fiery arrows.
Comment: There is only *one true God*.

24

Who Is the One True God?

There is only one God and no other, and if I am to describe what I think God is, then it would be a described below:

- a God is without sin;
- God is the same yesterday, today, and tomorrow;
- existed before time and for eternity;
- has authority over death and sin;
- judges righteously and sits on the throne of mercy;
- loves mankind not just in a general way but must declare it and prove it;
- hears the cries of mankind and answers;
- God is not dead and talks with his people in various ways;
- truly knows what it is to be human with all its frailties;
- God is living and not an inanimate object, and therefore communicates with mankind;
- is merciful, full of grace, and provides mankind a way out of death and hell;
- God is the embodiment of holiness and righteous, and cannot do otherwise;
- God is a supreme and transcends time and space;
- looks after those who believe and obey His Word;
- has a plan and forewarns mankind of the peril to come;

- shows His believers how to live without fear and superstitions;
- has authority over Satan, demons, and evil spirits;
- knows what you want even before you ask, and has a plan for you and your future;
- does not require man to have mindless repetitive chants and prayers in order to receive man's requests or cry; and
- God is all-powerful and have absolute command and authority over all the elements, molecules, atoms, and DNA, etc.

That is my perception of God and all His attributes, and is embodiment of holiness, mercy, righteousness, love, and grace. God talks with His creation, and is that the same for you?

The question is, do you want any lesser for a supreme and almighty God?

Christian Doctrine on Idol Worship

Leviticus 19:4: "Do not turn to **idols or make for yourselves molten gods**; I am the LORD your God."

Leviticus 26:1: "You shall not make for yourselves **idols**, nor shall you set up for yourselves **an image or a sacred pillar**, nor shall you place **a figured stone** in your land to bow down to it; for I am the LORD your God."

Deuteronomy 32:19–21: "The LORD saw this, and spurned them Because of the provocation of His sons and daughters. Then He said, 'I will hide My face from them, I will see what their end shall be; For they are a perverse generation, Sons in whom is no faithfulness. **They have made Me jealous with what is not God; They have provoked Me to anger with their idols**. So I will make them jealous with those who are not a people; instead of provoking them to anger with a foolish nation.'"

25

Sin, the Nature of Mankind

In general, Buddhism does not believe in a god, and therefore does not recognize sin. To sin is to trespass against God and His Laws, and if there is no god, then there is no trespassing or sin. Buddhism goes to extreme to break down the different causes of what it calls or terms as *craving*. (1) Craving for sensual pleasure through the eye, ear, nose, mouth, touch, and mind, termed as Kama Tanha; (2) craving for becoming or the desire to live, termed as Bhava Tanha; and lastly (3) craving to escape from various unpleasant states, termed as Vibhava Tanha. When the craving arises, the mind directs the body to act in certain ways, and therefore all actions are directed by the mind. When the mind acts in ignorance or with *selfish intentions,* it produces results, like murder, that are karmically determined; that is called Akusla Karma. Such actions and intentions are out of ignorance, and there needs compassion and education and definitely not punishment. The result of Akusla Karma results in getting stuck in the endless Samsara cycle.

What all these mean is that in Buddhism, there is no punishment for the murderer but reeducation, and for the person that is killed, he or she will enter the Samsara cycle and return to another life depending in the good and bad merits accumulated over his or her lifetime. (However, some schools of Buddhism teach that there are many gruesome tortures for those that are dead and awaiting to be released from the Samsara cycle.) And for the relatives and spouse of the person murdered, it is just too bad, as it is just plain karma. A serial killer, rapist, or drug lord will have a field day, and the reason for that is because all that can happen to them is just going down a little lower in the Samsara cycle. And when the time is right, he or she, in another lifetime, will do good works to redeem him or herself to work his or her way back up the Samsara cycle. When there is no God, then there is no moral law, and mankind becomes a law unto himself or herself.

Buddhism had arrived with its own sets of guidelines, which will allow them to accumulate good merits, and thus good karma:

(i)   not to harm living beings;
(ii) nor to take anything not freely given;
(iii) not to indulge in sexual behaviour which harms or hurts oneself and others;
(iv) not to speak falsehood or to indulge in unprofitable talk or gossip; and
(v)   not to consume any substance which will cause lawlessness and cause one to break the other four restraints.

The above are just guidelines, and no one is forced to uphold them or is punished if it is not followed. All that meant is that the person who breaks the guidelines will possibly, after death, come back from a lower part of the Samsara cycle or that one can later compensate it by doing some good works.

It is indeed a strange thing to be able to do something bad, and then make up for it by doing something good with no thought as to the consequences, and there is no compensation to the parties hurt maybe because it is part of their karma.

In this basic teaching of Buddhism, it does not deal with the root of the *evil* that arises from within a person but wrestle to deal with the different aspects or fruits of darkness within a person. It ceaselessly struggles to suppress the *rising* from within by meditation and sheer force and strength by the will of *man*. It is an endless struggle because it does not deal with the root of *rising* or *craving*.

Buddhism is a religion of *pride* in believing that the strong will of *man* is capable and able to suppress all that comes from within; that is, his or her lusts, greed, cravings, sexual lusts, murder, hate, anger, power, control, etc. by meditation.

In as much as the claim that Buddhism is a religion of non-self, the irony is, the contrary is true because it is by the strong self that rises in meditation to try and defeat and suppress all the cravings and yearnings of the flesh for power, control, cravings, lust, hate, and anger. Even as it succeeds in temporarily suppressing one at any time, another rises and it becomes an endless time spent in meditation. Even as it thinks one is defeated, it will rise another day to the dismay of the meditator. The minute that one claims to have defeated all, the ugly head of pride comes in and slay the proclaimed victor, and the battle starts all over again. Now that if the meditator felt that he had slain all, he is now a Buddha, he acts humbly, and it is very different than being a truly humble person.

26

Christian Concept and Nature of Sin

Mankind is born with a nature to do good and bad, and he/she is driven by his nature to satisfy his/her fleshly, psychological, and mental needs, as well as his/her ego or self. Buddhism in its core belief suppresses what the Western world defines as "self" and hopes to arrive at a status of "non-self" existence.

Mankind is compelled to do whatever he/she wanted to satisfy the wants, needs, and desires. Without any guidelines or the framework of law, the man only wreaks havoc in all that he/she does where only the strongest and most powerful controls most things. Buddhism, Islam, or Hinduism did not come up with a list of a moral code of conduct.

Even before the arrival of Moses and the Ten Commandments, the statutes, and ordinances that God gave him for the people around 1446 BC, God had created and given mankind conscience.

Out of that conscience came rulers and wise counsellors that arrived at a set of *laws* for society to live by. Before the Mosaic Law, the earlier discovered laws to date are those of the Mesopotamian civilization: 1. Code or Ur-Nammu, king of Ur (~2050 BC); 2. Laws of Eshnunna (~1930 BC); 3. Codex of Lipit-Ishtar (~1870 BC); and 4. Laws of Hammurabi (1792–1750 BC). Previous to the Mosaic Law, all the laws were man-made in order to bring a sense of law and order to the communities they live in. During the period before Moses, all the civilizations were worshipping pantheons of gods and idols and over all manners of sacrifices, and that is what happens when mankind is left to his own devices and intellect. It is out of that time period, around 1800 BC, a man named Abraham of Ur was called by God to serve His purpose in preparing a people to serve Him and deliver His message to the world. It is from Abraham's descendants that Moses was chosen by God to deliver His sets or laws, ordinances, and statutes to the people of His choosing. As a result, the trespass of the God's law is *sin* against God. *Read what the Ten Commandments given by God to Moses for all people as found in Exodus 20:1–26 (~1800 BC),*

> Then God spoke all these words, saying, "I am the Lord your God, who brought you out of the land of Egypt, out of the house of slavery. You shall have no other gods before Me.
>
> You shall not make for yourself an idol, or any likeness of what is in heaven above or on the earth beneath or in the water under the earth. You shall not worship them or serve them; for I, the Lord your God, am a jealous God, visiting the iniquity of the fathers on the children, on the third and the fourth generations of those who hate Me, but showing loving kindness to thousands, to those who love Me and keep My commandments.
>
> You shall not take the name of the Lord your God in vain, for the Lord will not leave him unpunished who takes His name in vain.
>
> Remember the sabbath day, to keep it holy. Six days you shall labor and do all your work, but the seventh day is a sabbath of the Lord your God; in it you shall not do any work, you or your son or your daughter, your male or your female servant or your cattle or your sojourner who stays with you. For in six days the Lord made the heavens and the earth, the sea and all that is in them,

and rested on the seventh day; therefore the Lord blessed the sabbath day and made it holy.

Honour your father and your mother, that your days may be prolonged in the land which the Lord your God gives you.

You shall not murder.

You shall not commit adultery.

You shall not steal.

You shall not bear false witness against your neighbour.

You shall not covet your neighbour's house; you shall not covet your neighbour's wife or his male servant or his female servant or his ox or his donkey or anything that belongs to your neighbour."

All the people perceived the thunder and the lightning flashes and the sound of the trumpet and the mountain smoking; and when the people saw it, they trembled and stood at a distance. Then they said to Moses, "Speak to us yourself and we will listen; but let not God speak to us, or we will die." Moses said to the people, "Do not be afraid; for God has come in order to test you, and in order that the fear of Him may remain with you, so that you may not sin." So the people stood at a distance, while Moses approached the thick cloud where God was. Then the LORD said to Moses, "Thus you shall say to the sons of Israel, You yourselves have seen that I have spoken to you from heaven. You shall not make other gods besides Me; gods of silver or gods of gold, you shall not make for yourselves. You shall make an altar of earth for Me, and you shall sacrifice on it your burnt offerings and your peace offerings, your sheep and your oxen; in every place where I cause My name to be remembered, I will come to you and bless you. If you make an altar of stone for Me, you shall not build it of cut stones, for if you wield your tool on it, you will profane it. And you shall not go up by steps to My altar, so that your nakedness will not be exposed on it."

Here in these sacred scriptures, God tells the people that there is only one God and no one else and Him only shall the people worship.

Other than the Ten Commandments, there were over six hundred statutes and ordinances that were given to the people of Israel to observe. *So the breaking or trespass of any one of the laws is sin before God. It is God's laws, and it is Him you have offended in the first place, and therefore only He can forgive you your sins!*

James 2:10 (~AD 62) says, "For whoever keeps the whole law and yet stumbles in one point, he has become guilty of all."

The family (seventy members) of Jacob fled the famine in the land of Canaan and lived in Egypt (1800 BC) with Jacob's son, Joseph, who was a high official of the Pharaoh in Egypt. But they suffered as slaves under the new Pharaohs for four hundred years. Moses was chosen by God at the age of eighty to lead the people out of their suffering and return to the promised land of Canaan. The exodus started around 1446 BC, and the people wandered in the desert for forty years because of sin. During the time of wandering in the desert, God gave the Ten Commandments, ordinances, and statutes, as well as instructions of sacrifices for sins and instructions for the construction of the tabernacle to the people through Moses. Moses, because of disobedience, did not enter into the promised land of Canaan, but it was Joshua and Caleb who led the people into the promised land.

27

Sin

A. All Have Sinned

Romans 3:21–24 (~AD 30–55) says, "But now apart from the Law the righteousness of God has been manifested, being witnessed by the Law and the Prophets, even the righteousness of God through faith in Jesus Christ for all those who believe; for there is no distinction; for all have sinned and fall short of the glory of God, being justified as a gift by His grace through the redemption which is in Christ Jesus."

B. Slave of Sin

John 8:34 (~AD 30–90) says, "Jesus answered them, 'Truly, truly, I say to you, everyone who commits sin is the slave of sin.'"

Comments: The Buddhists recognize all the many diverse and various sins, and that they are a slave to sin but elect to overcome it by meditation and suppress all their *cravings*! Whereas in Christianity, the *sin* nature of *man* is dealt with by the crucifixion of Jesus on the cross. Buddhism also recognizes that a person or man cannot overcome sin in a lifetime, and therefore takes many years, even hundreds of years, by going through the Samsara cycle of rebirths to continually improve his or her lot until man achieves Nirvana. But then again, Buddhism has no clear definition of or is vague about Nirvana or what actually happens in Nirvana. However, Tibetan and some schools of Mahayana Buddhism teach that it has superior meditation techniques that allow its follower to achieve Nirvana in one lifetime.

C. Wages of Sin

Romans 6:23 (~AD 30–55) says, "For the wages of sin is death, but the free gift of God is eternal life in Christ Jesus our Lord."

The apostle Paul wrote the epistle or letter to the Romans and is one of the most profound and important in Christian doctrine. It explained how mankind is under bondage or slavery to sin under the law, and how the law of the spirit of life through Jesus Christ sets us free. It is like gravity where everyone is subjected to it, and it is the law of aerodynamics that sets us free from the law of gravity. Not only do we receive eternal life when we accept Jesus, the Son of God, who was crucified on the cross and then resurrected from the dead, but that the Spirit of God sets us free from bondage to sin and the flesh.

28

Humanity's Struggle

A. What Is Sin?

First John 5:17 (~AD 30–90) says, "All unrighteousness is sin."

Psalm 89:32 (~1035–961 BC) says, "Then I will punish their transgression with the rod and their iniquity with stripes."

Comment: The scriptures here defined that transgression against God's law and iniquity is sin. God gave the people through His prophet Moses the Ten Commandments and some six hundred plus statutes and ordinances to keep.

B. Man's Struggle with Sin

Romans 6:4–23 (~AD 30–55) says,

> Therefore we have been buried with Him through baptism into death, so that as Christ was raised from the dead through the glory of the Father, so we too might walk in newness of life. For if we have become united with Him in the likeness of His death, certainly we shall also be in the likeness of His resurrection, knowing this, that our old self was crucified with Him, in order that our body of sin might be done away with, so

that we would no longer be slaves to sin; for he who has died is freed from sin. Now if we have died with Christ, we believe that we shall also live with Him, knowing that Christ, having been raised from the dead, is never to die again; death no longer is master over Him. For the death that He died, He died to sin once for all; but the life that He lives, He lives to God. Even so consider yourselves to be dead to sin, but alive to God in Christ Jesus. Therefore do not let sin reign in your mortal body so that you obey its lusts, and do not go on presenting the members of your body to sin as instruments of unrighteousness; but present yourselves to God as those alive from the dead, and your members as instruments of righteousness to God. For sin shall not be master over you, for you are not under law but under grace. What then? Shall we sin because we are not under law but under grace? May it never be! Do you not know that when you present yourselves to someone as slaves for obedience, you are slaves of the one whom you obey, either of sin result- ing in death, or of obedience resulting in righ- teousness? But thanks be to God that though you were slaves of sin, you became obedient from the heart to that form of teaching to which you were committed, and having been freed from sin, you became slaves of righteousness. I am speaking in human terms because of the weakness of your flesh. For just as you presented your members as slaves to impurity and to lawlessness, resulting in further lawlessness, so now present your members as slaves to righteousness, resulting in sanctifica- tion. For when you were slaves of sin, you were free in regard to righteousness. Therefore what benefit were you then deriving from the things of which you are now ashamed? For the outcome of those things is death. But now having been freed from sin and enslaved to God, you derive your benefit, resulting in sanctification, and the outcome, eternal life. For the wages of sin is death, but the free gift of God is eternal life in Christ Jesus our Lord.

C. The Struggle When Under the Law

Romans 7:1–25 (~AD 30–55) says,

> Or do you not know, brethren (for I am speaking to those who know the law), that the law has jurisdiction over a person as long as he lives? For the married woman is bound by law to her husband while he is living; but if her husband dies, she is released from the law concerning the husband. So then, if while her husband is living she is joined to another man, she shall be called an adulteress; but if her husband dies, she is free from the law, so that she is not an adulteress though she is joined to another man. Therefore, my brethren, you also were made to die to the Law through the body of Christ, so that you might be joined to another, to Him who was raised from the dead, in order that we might bear fruit for God. For while we were in the flesh, the sinful passions, which were aroused by the Law, were at work in the members of our body to bear fruit for death. But now we have been released from the Law, having died to that by which we were bound, so that we serve in newness of the Spirit and not in oldness of the letter. What shall we say then? Is the Law sin? May it never be! On the contrary, I would not have come to know sin

except through the Law; for I would not have known about coveting if the Law had not said, "*You shall not covet.*" But sin, taking opportunity through the commandment, produced in me coveting of every kind; for apart from the Law sin is dead. I was once alive apart from the Law; but when the commandment came, sin became alive and I died; and this commandment, which was to result in life, proved to result in death for me; for sin, taking an opportunity through the commandment, deceived me and through it killed me. So then, the Law is holy, and the commandment is holy and righteous and good. Therefore did that which is good become a cause of death for me? May it never be! Rather it was sin, in order that it might be shown to be sin by effecting my death through that which is good, so that through the commandment sin would become utterly sinful. For we know that the Law is spiritual, but I am of flesh, sold into bondage to sin. For what I am doing, I do not understand; for I am not practicing what I would like to do, but I am doing the very thing I hate. But if I do the very thing I do not want to do, I agree with the Law, confessing that the Law is good. So now, no longer am I the one doing it, but sin, which dwells in me. For I know that nothing good dwells in me, that is, in my flesh; for the willing is present in me, but the doing of the good is not. For the good that I want, I do not do, but I practice the very evil that I do not want. But if I am doing the very thing I do not want, I am no longer the one doing it, but sin which dwells in me. I find then the principle that evil is present in me, the one who wants to do good. For I joyfully concur with the law of God in the inner man, but I see a different law in the members of my body, waging war against the law of my mind and making me a prisoner of the law of sin which is in my members. Wretched man that I am! Who will set me free from the body of this death? Thanks be to God through Jesus Christ our Lord! So then, on the one hand I myself with my mind am serving the law of God, but on the other, with my flesh the law of sin.

D. Jesus Sets You Free from the Curse of the Law

Romans 8:1–17 (~AD 30–55) says,

Therefore there is now no condemnation for those who are in Christ Jesus. *For the law of the Spirit of life in Christ Jesus has set you free from the law of sin and of death.* For what the Law could not do, weak as it was through the flesh, God did: sending His own Son in the likeness of sinful flesh and as an offering for sin, He condemned sin in the flesh, so that the requirement of the Law might be fulfilled in us, who do not walk according to the flesh but according to the Spirit. For those who are according to the flesh set their minds on the things of the flesh, but those who are according to the Spirit, the things of the Spirit. For the mind set on the flesh is death, but the mind set on the Spirit is life and peace, because the mind set on the flesh is hostile toward God; for it does not subject itself to the law of God, for it is not even able to do so, and those who are in the flesh cannot please God. However, you are not in the flesh but in the Spirit, if indeed the Spirit of God dwells in you. But if anyone does not have the Spirit of Christ, he does not belong to Him. If Christ is in you, though the body is dead because of sin, yet the spirit is alive because of righteousness. But if the Spirit of Him who raised Jesus from the dead dwells in you, He who raised Christ Jesus from the dead will also give life to your mortal bodies through His Spirit who dwells in you. So then, brethren, we are under obligation, not to the flesh, to live according to the flesh—for if you are living according to the flesh, you must die; but if by the Spirit you are putting to death the deeds of the body, you will live. For all who are being led by the Spirit of God, these are sons of God. For you have not received a spirit of slavery leading to fear again, but you have received a spirit of adoption as sons by which we cry out, "Abba! Father!" The Spirit Himself testifies with our spirit that we are children of God, and if children, heirs also, heirs of God and fellow heirs with Christ, if indeed we suffer with Him so that we may also be glorified with Him.

Galatians 5:16–25 (~AD 30–50) says,

But I say, walk by the Spirit, and you will not carry out the desire of the flesh. For the flesh sets its desire against the Spirit, and the Spirit against the flesh; for these are in opposition to one another, so that you may not do the things that you please. But if you are led by the Spirit, you are not under the Law. Now the deeds of the flesh are evident, which are: immorality, impurity, sensuality, idolatry, sorcery, enmities, strife, jealousy, outbursts of anger, disputes, dissensions, factions, envying, drunkenness, carousing, and things like these, of which I forewarn you, just as I have forewarned you, that those who practice such things will not inherit the kingdom of God. But the fruit of the Spirit is love, joy, peace, patience, kindness, goodness, faithfulness, gentleness, self-control; against such things there is no law. Now those who belong to Christ Jesus have crucified the flesh with its passions and desires. If we live by the Spirit, let us also walk by the Spirit.

The Epistle to the Galatians is a letter written by the Apostle Paul to the Christian communities living in Galatia, Turkey. The original was written around AD 50, in papyrus, and only fragments were found and preserved.

E. Grafted into The True Vine, Jesus Christ

John 15:1–5 (~AD 30–90) says,

I am the true vine, and My Father is the vinedresser. Every branch in Me that does not bear fruit, He takes away; and every branch that bears fruit, He prunes it so that it may bear more fruit. You are already clean because of the word which I have spoken to you. Abide in Me, and I in you. As the branch cannot bear fruit of itself unless it abides in the vine, so neither can you unless you abide in Me. I am the vine, you are the branches; he who abides in Me and I in him, he bears much fruit, for apart from Me you can do nothing.

Romans 11:17–24 (~AD 30–55) says,

But if some of the branches were broken off, and you, being a wild olive, were grafted in

among them and became partaker with them of
the rich root of the olive tree, do not be arro-
gant toward the branches; but if you are arro-
gant, remember that it is not you who supports
the root, but the root supports you. You will say
then, 'Branches were broken off so that I might
be grafted in.' Quite right, they were broken off
for their unbelief, but you stand by your faith.
Do not be conceited, but fear; for if God did not
spare the natural branches, He will not spare you,
either. Behold then the kindness and severity of
God; to those who fell, severity, but to you, God's
kindness, if you continue in His kindness; otherwise you also will be cut off. And they also, if
they do not continue in their unbelief, will be
grafted in, for God is able to graft them in again.
For if you were cut off from what is by nature
a wild olive tree, and were grafted contrary to
nature into a cultivated olive tree, how much
more will these who are the natural branches be
grafted into their own olive tree?

F. Come into the Blessing

(i) Indwelling of the Spirit of God That No One Can Take
Away
    Acts 13:52 (~AD 30–74) says, "And the disciples were
continually filled with joy and with the Holy Spirit."

(ii) Eternal Life (Life after Death) and Not Come Under
Judgment and Condemned
    John 3:16–18 says, "For God so loved the world, that
He gave His only begotten Son, that whoever believes in
Him shall not perish, but have eternal life. For God did not
send the Son into the world to judge the world, but that
the world might be saved through Him. He who believes

in Him is not judged; he who does not believe has been judged already, because he has not believed in the name of the only begotten Son of God."

(iii) Love of God

First John 4:7–13 (~AD 30–90) says, "Beloved, let us love one another, for love is from God; and everyone who loves is born of God and knows God. The one who does not love does not know God, for God is love. By this the love of God was manifested in us, that God has sent His only begotten Son into the world so that we might live through Him. In this is love, not that we loved God, but that He loved us and sent His Son to be the propitiation for our sins. Beloved, if God so loved us, we also ought to love one another. No one has seen God at any time; if we love one another, God abides in us, and His love is perfected in us. By this we know that we abide in Him and He in us, because He has given us of His Spirit."

Romans 8:37–39 (~AD 30–55) says, "But in all these things we overwhelmingly conquer through Him who loved us. For I am convinced that neither death, nor life, nor angels, nor principalities, nor things present, nor things to come, nor powers, nor height, nor depth, nor any other created thing, will be able to separate us from the love of God, which is in Christ Jesus our Lord."

(iv) Joy and Peace

Galatians 5:22–23 (~AD 30–50) says, "But the fruit of the Spirit is love, joy, peace, patience, kindness, goodness, faithfulness, gentleness, self-control; against such things there is no law."

John 15:11 says, "These things I have spoken to you so that My joy may be in you, and that your joy may be made full."

Romans 15:13 says, "And the disciples were continually filled with joy and with the Holy Spirit."

29

Christian Doctrine on Forgiveness

A. God's Provision for Forgiveness in the *Old Covenant*: An Animal Sacrifice for Sin

Hebrews 9:22 (~AD 64) says, "And according to the Law, one may almost say, all things are cleansed with blood, and without shedding of blood there is no forgiveness. According to the Old Testament of the Bible there are many kinds of sin offerings before God. Here is an example of one of them."

Leviticus 4:1–20 (~1445 BC) says,

> Then the Lord spoke to Moses, saying, "Speak to the sons of Israel, saying, 'If a person sins unintentionally in any of the things which the Lord has commanded not to be done, and commits any of them, if the anointed priest sins so as to bring guilt on the people, then let him offer to the Lord a bull without defect as a sin offering for the sin he has committed. He shall bring the bull to the doorway of the tent of meeting before the Lord, and he shall lay his hand on the head of the bull and slay the bull before the Lord. Then the anointed priest is to take some of the blood of the bull and bring it to the tent of

meeting, and the priest shall dip his finger in the blood and sprinkle some of the blood seven times before the Lord, in front of the veil of the sanctuary. The priest shall also put some of the blood on the horns of the altar of fragrant incense which is before the Lord in the tent of meeting; and all the blood of the bull he shall pour out at the base of the altar of burnt offering which is at the doorway of the tent of meeting. He shall remove from it all the fat of the bull of the sin offering: the fat that covers the entrails, and all the fat which is on the entrails, and the two kidneys with the fat that is on them, which is on the loins, and the lobe of the liver, which he shall remove with the kidneys (just as it is removed from the ox of the sacrifice of peace offerings), and the priest is to offer them up in smoke on the altar of burnt offering. But the hide of the bull and all its flesh with its head and its legs and its entrails and its refuse, that is, all the rest of the bull, he is to bring out to a clean place outside the camp where the ashes are poured out, and burn it on wood with fire; where the ashes are poured out it shall be burned. Now if the whole congregation of Israel commits error and the matter escapes the notice of the assembly, and they commit any of the things which the Lord has commanded not to be done, and they become guilty; when the sin which they have committed becomes known, then the assembly shall offer a bull of the herd for a sin offering and bring it before the tent of meeting. Then the elders of the congregation shall lay their hands on the head of the bull before the Lord, and the bull shall be slain before the Lord. Then the anointed priest is to bring some of the blood of the bull to the tent of meeting; and the priest shall dip his finger in the blood and sprinkle it seven times before the Lord, in front of the veil. He shall put some of the blood on the horns of the altar which is before the Lord in the tent of meeting; and all the blood he shall pour out at the base of the altar of burnt offering which is at the doorway of the tent of meeting. He shall remove all its fat from it and offer it up in smoke on the altar. He shall also do with the bull just as he did with the bull of the sin offering; thus he shall do with it. So the priest shall make atonement for them, and they will be forgiven.'"

B. God's Provision for Forgiveness in the *New Covenant*

God offered up His Begotten Son as a sacrifice for sin for all people, once and forever as stated in *Hebrews 10:16–18*, "'*This is the covenant that I will make with them after those days, says the lord: I will put my laws upon their heart, and on their mind I will write them,*' He then says, '*And their sins and their lawless deeds I will remember no more.*' Now where there is forgiveness of these things, there is no longer any offering for sin."

(i)   The Prophecy of the Birth of God's Son *Isaiah 7:14 (~740–698 BC)* says, "Therefore the Lord Himself will give you a sign: Behold, a virgin will be with child and bear a son, and she will call His name Immanuel."

The Fulfilment of the Prophecy

Matthew 1:18–2:10 (~AD 30–60) says,

Now the birth of Jesus Christ was as follows: when His mother Mary had been betrothed to Joseph, before they came together she was found to be with child by the Holy Spirit. And

Joseph her husband, being a righteous man and not wanting to disgrace her, planned to send her away secretly. But when he had considered this, behold, an angel of the Lord appeared to him in a dream, saying, "Joseph, son of David, do not be afraid to take Mary as your wife; for the Child who has been conceived in her is of the Holy Spirit. She will bear a Son; and you shall call His name Jesus, for He will save His people from their sins." Now all this took place to fulfill what was spoken by the Lord through the prophet: *"Behold, the virgin shall be with child and shall bear a son, and they shall call his name Immanuel,"* which translated means, *"God with us."* And Joseph awoke from his sleep and did as the angel of the Lord commanded him, and took Mary as his wife, but kept her a virgin until she gave birth to a Son; and he called His name Jesus.

Now after Jesus was born in Bethlehem of Judea in the days of Herod the king, magi from the east arrived in Jerusalem, saying, "Where is He who has been born King of the Jews? For we saw His star in the east and have come to worship Him." When Herod the king heard this, he was troubled, and all Jerusalem with him. Gathering together all the chief priests and scribes of the people, he inquired of them where the Messiah was to be born. They said to him, "In Bethlehem of Judea; for this is what has been written by the prophet: *'And you, Bethlehem, land of Judah, are by no means least among the leaders of Judah; for out of you shall come forth a ruler who will shepherd my people Israel.'"* Then Herod secretly called the magi and determined from them the exact time the star appeared. And he sent them to Bethlehem and said, "Go and search carefully for the Child;

and when you have found Him, report to me, so that I too may come and worship Him." After hearing the king, they went their way; and the star, which they had seen in the east, went on before them until it came and stood over the place where the Child was. When they saw the star, they rejoiced exceedingly with great joy.

(ii) The Prophecy of His Suffering and Crucifixion

Isaiah 50:6 (~740–698 BC) says, "I gave My back to those who strike Me, And My cheeks to those who pluck out the beard; I did not cover My face from humiliation and spitting."
Isaiah 53:1–7 says,

> Who has believed our message? And to whom has the arm of the Lord been revealed? For He grew up before Him like a tender shoot, And like a root out of parched ground; He has no stately form or majesty That we should look upon Him, Nor appearance that we should be attracted to Him. He was despised and forsaken of men, A man of sorrows and acquainted with grief; And like one from whom men hide their face He was despised, and we did not esteem Him. Surely our griefs He Himself bore, And our sorrows He carried; Yet we ourselves esteemed Him stricken, Smitten of God, and afflicted. But He was pierced through for our transgressions, He was crushed for our iniquities; The chastening for our well-being fell upon Him, And by His scourging we are healed. All of us like sheep have gone astray, Each of us has turned to his own way; But the Lord has caused the iniquity of us all To fall on Him. He was oppressed and He was afflicted, Yet He did not open His mouth; Like

a lamb that is led to slaughter, And like a sheep that is silent before its shearers, So He did not open His mouth.

The Fulfilment of the Prophecy

John 18:12–19:37 (~AD 30–90) says,

> So the Roman cohort and the commander and the officers of the Jews, arrested Jesus and bound Him, and led Him to Annas first; for he was father-in-law of Caiaphas, who was high priest that year. Now Caiaphas was the one who had advised the Jews that it was expedient for one man to die on behalf of the people. Simon Peter was following Jesus, and so was another disciple. Now that disciple was known to the high priest, and entered with Jesus into the court of the high priest, but Peter was standing at the door outside. So the other disciple, who was known to the high priest, went out and spoke to the doorkeeper, and brought Peter in. Then the slave-girl who kept the door said to Peter, "You are not also one of this man's disciples, are you?" He said, "I am not." Now the slaves and the officers were standing there, having made a charcoal fire, for it was cold and they were warming themselves; and Peter was also with them, standing and warming himself. The high priest then questioned Jesus about His disciples, and about His teaching. Jesus answered him, "I have spoken openly to the world; I always taught in synagogues and in the temple, where all the Jews come together; and I spoke nothing in secret. Why do you question Me? Question those who have heard what I spoke to them; they know what I said." When He had

said this, one of the officers standing nearby struck Jesus, saying, "Is that the way You answer the high priest?" Jesus answered him, "If I have spoken wrongly, testify of the wrong; but if rightly, why do you strike Me?" So Annas sent Him bound to Caiaphas the high priest. Now Simon Peter was standing and warming himself. So they said to him, "You are not also one of His disciples, are you?" He denied it, and said, "I am not.' One of the slaves of the high priest, being a relative of the one whose ear Peter cut off, said, "Did I not see you in the garden with Him?" Peter then denied it again, and immediately a rooster crowed. Then they led Jesus from Caiaphas into the Praetorium, and it was early; and they themselves did not enter into the Praetorium so that they would not be defiled, but might eat the Passover. Therefore Pilate went out to them and said, "What accusation do you bring against this Man?" They answered and said to him, "If this Man were not an evildoer, we would not have delivered Him to you." So Pilate said to them, "Take Him yourselves, and judge Him according to your law." The Jews said to him, "We are not permitted to put anyone to death," to fulfill the word of Jesus which He spoke, signifying by what kind of death He was about to die. Therefore Pilate entered again into the Praetorium, and summoned Jesus and said to Him, "Are You the King of the Jews?" Jesus answered, "Are you saying this on your own initiative, or did others tell you about Me?" Pilate answered, "I am not a Jew, am I? Your own nation and the chief priests delivered You to me; what have You done?" Jesus answered, "My kingdom is not of this world. If My kingdom were of this

world, then My servants would be fighting so
that I would not be handed over to the Jews; but
as it is, My kingdom is not of this realm."
Therefore Pilate said to Him, "So You are a king?"
Jesus answered, "You say correctly that I am a
king. For this I have been born, and for this I
have come into the world, to testify to the truth.
Everyone who is of the truth hears My voice."
Pilate said to Him, "What is truth?" And when
he had said this, he went out again to the Jews
and said to them, "I find no guilt in Him. But
you have a custom that I release someone for you
at the Passover; do you wish then that I release for
you the King of the Jews?" So they cried out
again, saying, "Not this Man, but Barabbas."
Now Barabbas was a robber. Pilate then took
Jesus and scourged Him. And the soldiers twisted
together a crown of thorns and put it on His
head, and put a purple robe on Him; and they
began to come up to Him and say, "Hail, King of
the Jews!" and to give Him slaps in the face. Pilate
came out again and said to them, "Behold, I am
bringing Him out to you so that you may know
that I find no guilt in Him." Jesus then came out,
wearing the crown of thorns and the purple robe.
Pilate said to them, "Behold, the Man!" So when
the chief priests and the officers saw Him, they
cried out saying, "Crucify, crucify!" Pilate said to
them, "Take Him yourselves and crucify Him,
for I find no guilt in Him." The Jews answered
him, "We have a law, and by that law He ought
to die because He made Himself out to be the
Son of God." Therefore when Pilate heard this
statement, he was even more afraid; and he
entered into the Praetorium again and said to
Jesus, "Where are You from?" But Jesus gave him

no answer. So Pilate said to Him, "You do not speak to me? Do You not know that I have authority to release You, and I have authority to crucify You?" Jesus answered, "You would have no authority over Me, unless it had been given you from above; for this reason he who delivered Me to you has the greater sin." As a result of this Pilate made efforts to release Him, but the Jews cried out saying, "If you release this Man, you are no friend of Caesar; everyone who makes himself out to be a king opposes Caesar." Therefore when Pilate heard these words, he brought Jesus out, and sat down on the judgment seat at a place called The Pavement, but in Hebrew, Gabbatha. Now it was the day of preparation for the Passover; it was about the sixth hour. And he said to the Jews, "Behold, your King!" So they cried out, "Away with Him, away with Him, crucify Him!" Pilate said to them, "Shall I crucify your King?" The chief priests answered, "We have no king but Caesar." So he then handed Him over to them to be crucified. They took Jesus, therefore, and He went out, bearing His own cross, to the place called the Place of a Skull, which is called in Hebrew, Golgotha. There they crucified Him, and with Him two other men, one on either side, and Jesus in between. Pilate also wrote an inscription and put it on the cross. It was written, *"Jesus the Nazarene, the King of the Jews."* Therefore many of the Jews read this inscription, for the place where Jesus was crucified was near the city; and it was written in Hebrew, Latin and in Greek. So the chief priests of the Jews were saying to Pilate, "Do not write, 'The King of the Jews'; but that He said, 'I am King of the Jews.'" Pilate answered, "What I have written I have written."

147

Then the soldiers, when they had crucified Jesus, took His outer garments and made four parts, a part to every soldier and also the tunic; now the tunic was seamless, woven in one piece. So they said to one another, "Let us not tear it, but cast lots for it, to decide whose it shall be"; this was to fulfill the Scripture: *They divided my outer garments among them, and for my clothing they cast lots.* " Therefore the soldiers did these things. But standing by the cross of Jesus were His mother, and His mother's sister, Mary the wife of Clopas, and Mary Magdalene. When Jesus then saw His mother, and the disciple whom He loved standing nearby, He said to His mother, "Woman, behold, your son!" Then He said to the disciple, "Behold, your mother!" From that hour the disciple took her into his own household. After this, Jesus, knowing that all things had already been accomplished, to fulfill the Scripture, said, "I am thirsty." A jar full of sour wine was standing there; so they put a sponge full of the sour wine upon a branch of hyssop and brought it up to His mouth. Therefore when Jesus had received the sour wine, He said, "It is finished!" And He bowed His head and gave up His spirit. Then the Jews, because it was the day of preparation, so that the bodies would not remain on the cross on the Sabbath (for that Sabbath was a high day), asked Pilate that their legs might be broken, and that they might be taken away. So the soldiers came, and broke the legs of the first man and of the other who was crucified with Him; but coming to Jesus, when they saw that He was already dead, they did not break His legs. But one of the soldiers pierced His side with a spear, and immediately blood and water came out. And he who has seen has testified, and his testimony is true; and he knows that he is telling the truth, so that you also may believe. For these things came to pass to fulfill the Scripture, *"Not a bone of him shall be broken."* And, again, another scripture says, *"They shall look on him whom they pierced."*

Psalms 22:12–18 (~1035–961) says,

Many bulls have surrounded me; Strong bulls of Bashan have encircled me. They open wide their mouth at me, As a ravening and a roaring lion. I am poured out like water, And all my bones are out of joint; My heart is like wax; It is melted within me. My strength is dried up like a potsherd, and my tongue cleaves to my jaws; And You lay me in the dust of death. For dogs have surrounded me; A band of evildoers has encompassed me; They pierced my hands and my feet. I can count all my bones. They look, they stare at me; They divide my garments among them, And for my clothing they cast lots.

(iii) The Prophecy of his Resurrection

Psalms 16:10 (~1035–961 BC) says, "For You will not abandon my soul to Sheol; Nor will You allow Your Holy One to undergo decay."

The Fulfilment of the Prophecy

John 20:1–17 (~AD 30–90) says,

Now on the first day of the week Mary Magdalene came early to the tomb, while it was still dark, and saw the stone already taken away from the tomb. So she ran and came to Simon Peter and to the other disciple whom Jesus loved, and said to them, "They have taken away the Lord out of the tomb, and we do not know where they have laid Him." So Peter and the other disciple went forth, and they were going to the tomb. The two were running together; and the other disciple ran ahead faster than Peter and came to the tomb first; and stooping and looking in, he saw the linen wrappings lying there; but he did not go in. And so Simon Peter also came, following him, and entered the tomb; and he saw the linen wrappings lying there, and the face-cloth which had been on His head, not lying with the linen wrappings, but rolled up in a place by itself. So the other disciple who had first come to the tomb then also entered, and he saw and believed. For as yet they did not understand the Scripture that He must rise again from the dead. So the disciples went away again to their own homes. But Mary was standing outside the tomb weeping; and so, as she wept, she stooped and looked into the tomb; and she saw two angels in white sitting, one at the head and one at the feet, where the body of Jesus had been lying. And they said to her, "Woman, why are you weeping?" She said to them, "Because they have taken away my Lord, and I do not know where they have laid Him." When she had said this, she turned around and saw Jesus standing there, and did not know that it was Jesus. Jesus said to her, "Woman, why are you weeping? Whom are you seeking?" Supposing Him to be the gardener, she said to Him, "Sir, if you have carried Him away, tell me where you have laid Him, and I will take Him away." Jesus said to her, "Mary!" She turned and said to Him in Hebrew, "Rabboni!" (which means Teacher). Jesus said to her, "Stop clinging to Me, for I have not yet ascended to the Father; but go to My brethren and say to them, I ascend to My Father and your Father, and My God and your God."

John 20:24–28 says,

> But Thomas, one of the twelve, called Didymus, was not with them when Jesus came. So the other disciples were saying to him, "We have seen the Lord!" But he said to them, "Unless I see in His hands the imprint of the nails, and put my finger into the place of the nails, and put my hand into His side, I will not believe." After eight days His disciples were again inside, and Thomas with them. Jesus came, the doors having been shut, and stood in their midst and said, "Peace be with you." Then He said to Thomas, "Reach here with your finger, and see My hands; and reach here your hand and put it into My side; and do not be unbelieving, but believing." Thomas answered and said to Him, *"My Lord and my God!"*

Comment: Buddhism believes that if anyone can forgive sins, it must be the person himself or herself and not someone external, and that good and bad deeds are done by the person himself or herself and is therefore responsible for the purity of his or her own mind. Buddhism does not believe in praying and worshipping God or asking God, for forgiveness is a reasonable action as there is no god. For those believing in God and the punishment of a permanent hell for sins, Buddhism believes they are superstitious, illogical, and motivated by fear out of ignorance of a better way.

30

Gautama Siddhartha, the Person

The person of Gautama was introduced earlier. He did not exhibit any extraordinary powers or the ability to prophesy. Gautama Siddhartha was just an ordinary person who tried to overcome all human cravings and sufferings by sheer strength of his will through meditation to suppress all those thoughts that arose in him. He is said to have succeeded and encouraged all to follow him. Only very few of the population is able to forsake all and follow his ways, as millions who called themselves Buddhists are stuck in the Samsara cycle. Absolutely no Buddhist knows what happened to Gautama Siddhartha or a few like him after they are reputed to have escaped the Samsara cycle, but there is no concrete evidence to support the supposition.

The whole Buddhist faith hangs on rumours and tales with no concrete evidence or proof. Why would anyone put their fate of their afterlife on rumours, suppositions, and superstitions? It is like putting your whole life in the hands of King Kong the giant gorilla to bring you a better life after death. You have to ask, does it really make any sense? Gautama Siddhartha only points to the way, but as for himself, he did not demonstrate any sense of authority or power over nature and mankind and have the power to perform miracles.

31

Jesus, the Begotten Son of God

Look at the documentation and testaments of what Jesus of Nazareth had done:

(i)   Jesus healing the blind in more than one instance.

Mark 10:46–52 (~AD 30–70) says,

> Then they came to Jericho. And as He was leaving Jericho with His disciples and a large crowd, a blind beggar named Bartimaeus, the son of Timaeus, was sitting by the road. When he heard that it was Jesus the Nazarene, he began to cry out and say, "Jesus, Son of David, have mercy on me!" Many were sternly telling him to be quiet, but he kept crying out all the more, "Son of David, have mercy on me!" And Jesus stopped and said, "Call him here." So they called the blind man, saying to him, "Take courage, stand up! He is calling for you." Throwing aside his cloak, he jumped up and came to Jesus. And answering him, Jesus said, "What do you want Me to do for you?" And the blind man said to Him, "Rabboni, I want to regain my sight!" And

Jesus said to him, "Go; your faith has made you well." Immediately he regained his sight and began following Him on the road.

(ii) Jesus's healing of lepers in more than one instance.

Mark 1:40–45 says,

> And a leper came to Jesus, beseeching Him and falling on his knees before Him, and saying, "If You are willing, You can make me clean." Moved with compassion, Jesus stretched out His hand and touched him, and said to him, "I am willing; be cleansed." Immediately the leprosy left him and he was cleansed. And He sternly warned him and immediately sent him away, and He said to him, "See that you say nothing to anyone; but go, show yourself to the priest and offer for your cleansing what Moses commanded, as a testimony to them." But he went out and began to proclaim it freely and to spread the news around, to such an extent that Jesus could no longer publicly enter a city, but stayed out in unpopulated areas; and they were coming to Him from everywhere.

(iii) Jesus's healing of a man suffering from paralysis.

Matthew 9:1–8 (~AD 30–60) says,

> Getting into a boat, Jesus crossed over the sea and came to His own city. And they brought to Him a paralytic lying on a bed. Seeing their faith, Jesus said to the paralytic, "Take courage, son; your sins are forgiven." And some of the scribes said to themselves, "This fellow blas-

phemes." And Jesus knowing their thoughts said, "Why are you thinking evil in your hearts? Which is easier, to say, 'Your sins are forgiven,' or to say, 'Get up, and walk?' But so that you may know that the Son of Man has authority on earth to forgive sins"—then He said to the paralytic, "Get up, pick up your bed and go home." And he got up and went home. But when the crowds saw this, they were awestruck, and glorified God, who had given such authority to men.

(iv) Jesus healing a woman with internal bleeding.

Mark 5:21–34 (~AD 30–70) says,

When Jesus had crossed over again in the boat to the other side, a large crowd gathered around Him; and so He stayed by the seashore. One of the synagogue officials named Jairus came up, and on seeing Him, fell at His feet and implored Him earnestly, saying, "My little daughter is at the point of death; please come and lay Your hands on her, so that she will get well and live." And He went off with him; and a large crowd was following Him and pressing in on Him. A woman who had had a hemorrhage for twelve years, and had endured much at the hands of many physicians, and had spent all that she had and was not helped at all, but rather had grown worse—after hearing about Jesus, she came up in the crowd behind Him and touched His cloak. For she thought, "If I just touch His garments, I will get well." Immediately the flow of her blood was dried up; and she felt in her body that she was healed of her affliction. Immediately Jesus, perceiving in Himself that the power proceeding from Him had gone forth, turned around in the crowd and said, "Who touched My garments?" And His disciples said to Him, "You see the crowd pressing in on You, and You say, "Who touched Me?" And He looked around to see the woman who had done this. But the woman fearing and trembling, aware of what had happened to her, came and fell down before Him and told Him the whole truth. And He said to her, "Daughter, your faith has made you well; go in peace and be healed of your affliction."

(v) Jesus's healing by the authority and power of His Words.

Matthew 8:5–13 (~AD 30–60) says,

And when Jesus entered Capernaum, a centurion came to Him, imploring Him, and saying, "Lord, my servant is lying paralyzed at home, fearfully tormented." Jesus said to him, "I will come and heal him." But the centurion said, "Lord, I am not worthy for You to come under my roof, but just say the word, and my servant will be healed. For I also am a man under authority, with soldiers under me; and I say to this one, 'Go!' and he goes, and to another, 'Come!' and he comes, and to my slave, 'Do this!' and he does it." Now when Jesus heard this, He marvelled and said to those who were following, "Truly I say to you, I have not found such great faith with anyone in Israel. I say to you that many will come from east and west, and recline at the table with Abraham, Isaac and Jacob in the kingdom of heaven; but the sons of the kingdom will be cast out into the outer darkness; in that place there will be weeping and gnashing of teeth." And Jesus said to the centurion, "Go; it shall be done for you as you have believed." And the servant was healed that very moment.

(vi) Jesus casting out demons.

Mark 5:1–20 (~AD 30–70) says,

> They came to the other side of the sea, into the country of the Gerasenes. When He got out of the boat, immediately a man from the tombs with an unclean spirit met Him, and he had his dwelling among the tombs. And no one was able to bind him anymore, even with a chain; because he had often been bound with shackles and chains, and the chains had been torn apart by him and the shackles broken in pieces, and no one was strong enough to subdue him. Constantly, night and day, he was screaming among the tombs and in the mountains, and gashing himself with stones. Seeing Jesus from a distance, he ran up and bowed down before Him; and shouting with a loud voice, he said, "What business do we have with each other, Jesus, Son of the Most High God? I implore You by God, do not torment me!" For He had been saying to him, "Come out of the man, you unclean spirit!" And He was asking him, "What is your name?" And he said to Him, "My name is Legion; for we are many." And he began to implore Him earnestly not to send them out of the country. Now there was a large herd of swine feeding nearby on the mountain. The demons implored Him, saying, "Send us into the swine so that we may enter them." Jesus gave them permission. And coming out, the unclean spirits entered the swine; and the herd

rushed down the steep bank into the sea, about
two thousand of them; and they were drowned in
the sea. Their herdsmen ran away and reported
it in the city and in the country. And the people came to see what it was that had happened.
They came to Jesus and observed the man who
had been demon-possessed sitting down, clothed
and in his right mind, the very man who had had
the "legion"; and they became frightened. Those
who had seen it described to them how it had
happened to the demon-possessed man, and all
about the swine. And they began to implore Him
to leave their region. As He was getting into the
boat, the man who had been demon-possessed
was imploring Him that he might accompany
Him. And He did not let him, but He said to
him, "Go home to your people and report to
them what great things the Lord has done for
you, and how He had mercy on you." And he
went away and began to proclaim in Decapolis
what great things Jesus had done for him; and
everyone was amazed.

(vii) Jesus's feeding of the five thousand men and families.

Matthew 14:13–21 (~AD 30–60) says,

Now when Jesus heard about John, He with-
drew from there in a boat to a secluded place by
Himself; and when the people heard of this, they
followed Him on foot from the cities. When He
went ashore, He saw a large crowd, and felt compassion for them and healed their sick. When it
was evening, the disciples came to Him and said,
"This place is desolate and the hour is already
late; so send the crowds away, that they may go

into the villages and buy food for themselves."
But Jesus said to them, "They do not need to
go away; you give them something to eat!" They
said to Him, "We have here only five loaves and
two fish." And He said, "Bring them here to Me."
Ordering the people to sit down on the grass, He
took the five loaves and the two fish, and looking up toward heaven, He blessed the food, and
breaking the loaves He gave them to the disciples, and the disciples gave them to the crowds,
and they all ate and were satisfied. They picked
up what was left over of the broken pieces, twelve
full baskets. There were about five thousand men
who ate, besides women and children.

(viii) Jesus raising the dead.

John 11:1–44 (~AD 30–90) says,

> Now a certain man was sick, Lazarus of
> Bethany, the village of Mary and her sister
> Martha. It was the Mary who anointed the Lord
> with ointment, and wiped His feet with her hair,
> whose brother Lazarus was sick. So the sisters
> sent word to Him, saying, "Lord, behold, he
> whom You love is sick." But when Jesus heard
> this, He said, "This sickness is not to end in
> death, but for the glory of God, so that the Son
> of God may be glorified by it." Now Jesus loved
> Martha and her sister and Lazarus. So when He
> heard that he was sick, He then stayed two days
> longer in the place where He was. Then after
> this He said to the disciples, "Let us go to Judea
> again." The disciples said to Him, "Rabbi, the
> Jews were just now seeking to stone You, and
> are You going there again?" Jesus answered, "Are

there not twelve hours in the day? If anyone walks in the day, he does not stumble, because he sees the light of this world. But if anyone walks in the night, he stumbles, because the light is not in him." This He said, and after that He said to them, "Our friend Lazarus has fallen asleep; but I go, so that I may awaken him out of sleep." The disciples then said to Him, "Lord, if he has fallen asleep, he will recover." Now Jesus had spoken of his death, but they thought that He was speaking of literal sleep. So Jesus then said to them plainly, "Lazarus is dead, and I am glad for your sakes that I was not there, so that you may believe; but let us go to him." Therefore Thomas, who is called Didymus, said to his fellow disciples, "Let us also go, so that we may die with Him." So when Jesus came, He found that he had already been in the tomb four days. Now Bethany was near Jerusalem, about two miles off; and many of the Jews had come to Martha and Mary, to console them concerning their brother. Martha therefore, when she heard that Jesus was coming, went to meet Him, but Mary stayed at the house. Martha then said to Jesus, "Lord, if You had been here, my brother would not have died. Even now I know that whatever You ask of God, God will give You." Jesus said to her, "Your brother will rise again." Martha said to Him, "I know that he will rise again in the resurrection on the last day." Jesus said to her, *"I am the resurrection and the life; he who believes in Me will live even if he dies, and everyone who lives and believes in Me will never die.* Do you believe this?" She said to Him, "Yes, Lord; I have believed that You are the Christ, the Son of God, even He who comes into the world." When she had said this, she went away and called Mary her sister, saying secretly, "The Teacher is here and is calling for you." And when she heard it, she got up quickly and was coming to Him. Now Jesus had not yet come into the village, but was still in the place where Martha met Him. Then the Jews who were with her in the house, and consoling her, when they saw that Mary got up quickly and went out, they followed her, supposing that she was going to the tomb to weep there. Therefore, when Mary came where Jesus was, she saw Him, and fell at His feet, saying to Him, "Lord, if You had been here, my brother would not have died." When Jesus therefore saw her weeping, and the Jews who came with her also weeping, He was deeply moved in spirit and was troubled, and said, "Where have you laid him?" They said to Him, "Lord, come and see." Jesus wept. So the Jews were saying, "See how He loved him!" But some of them said, "Could not this man, who opened the eyes of the blind man, have kept this man also from dying?" So Jesus, again being deeply moved within, came to the tomb. Now it was a cave, and a stone was lying against it. Jesus said, "Remove the stone." Martha, the sister of the deceased, said to Him, "Lord, by this time there will be a stench, for he has been dead four days." Jesus said to her, "Did I not say to you that if you believe, you will see the glory of God?" So they removed the stone. Then Jesus raised His eyes, and said, "Father, I thank You that You have heard Me. I knew that You always hear Me; but because of the people standing around I said it, so that they may believe that You sent Me." When He had said these things, He cried out with a loud voice,

"Lazarus, come forth." The man who had died came forth, bound hand and foot with wrappings, and his face was wrapped around with a cloth. Jesus said to them, "Unbind him, and let him go."

(ix) Jesus walked on water.

Matthew 14:22–33 (~AD 30–60) says,

Immediately He made the disciples get into the boat and go ahead of Him to the other side, while He sent the crowds away. After He had sent the crowds away, He went up on the mountain by Himself to pray; and when it was evening, He was there alone. But the boat was already a long distance from the land, battered by the waves; for the wind was contrary. And in the fourth watch of the night He came to them, walking on the sea. When the disciples saw Him walking on the sea, they were terrified, and said, "It is a ghost!" And they cried out in fear. But immediately Jesus spoke to them, saying, "Take courage, it is I; do not be afraid." Peter said to Him, "Lord, if it is You, command me to come to You on the water." And He said, "Come!" And Peter got out of the boat, and walked on the water and came toward Jesus. But seeing the wind, he became frightened, and beginning to sink, he cried out, "Lord, save me!" Immediately Jesus stretched out His hand and took hold of him, and said to him, "You of little faith, why did you doubt?" When they got into the boat, the wind stopped. And those who were in the boat worshiped Him, saying, "You are certainly God's Son!"

(x) Jesus rebuked the stormy sea.

Matthew 8:23–27 says,

When He got into the boat, His disciples followed Him. And behold, there arose a great storm on the sea, so that the boat was being covered with the waves; but Jesus Himself was asleep. And they came to Him and woke Him, saying, "Save us, Lord; we are perishing!" He said to them, "Why are you afraid, you men of little faith?" Then He got up and rebuked the winds and the sea, and it became perfectly calm. The men were amazed, and said, "What kind of a man is this, that even the winds and the sea obey Him?"

(xi) Jesus changing water into wine.

John 2:1–11 (~AD 30–90) says,

On the third day there was a wedding in Cana of Galilee, and the mother of Jesus was there; and both Jesus and His disciples were invited to the wedding. When the wine ran out, the mother of Jesus said to Him, "They have no wine." And Jesus said to her, "Woman, what does that have to do with us? My hour has not yet come." His mother said to the servants, "Whatever He says to you, do it." Now there were six stone waterpots set there for the Jewish custom of purification, containing twenty or thirty gallons each. Jesus said to them, "Fill the waterpots with water." So they filled them up to the brim. And He said to them, "Draw some out now and take it to the headwaiter." So they took it to him. When the headwaiter tasted the water which had become wine, and did not know where it came from (but the servants who had drawn the water knew), the headwaiter called the bridegroom, and said to him, "Every man serves the good wine first, and when the people have drunk freely, then he serves the poorer wine; but you have kept the good wine until now." This beginning of His signs Jesus did in Cana of Galilee, and manifested His glory, and His disciples believed in Him.

(xii) Jesus gave authority for His disciples to have the same power to heal and cast out demons.

Luke 9:1–2 (~AD 30–74) says, "And He called the twelve together, and gave them power and authority over all the demons and to heal diseases. And He sent them out to proclaim the kingdom of God and to perform healing."

John 14:12–14 says, "Truly, truly, I say to you, he who believes in Me, the works that I do, he will do also; and greater works than these he will do; because I go to the Father. Whatever you ask in My name, that will I do, so that the Father may be glorified in the Son. If you ask Me anything in My name, I will do it."

Acts 3:1–11 (~AD 30–74) says,

Now Peter and John were going up to the temple at the ninth hour, the hour of prayer. And a man who had been lame from his mother's womb was being carried along, whom they used to set down every day at the gate of the temple, which is called Beautiful, in order to beg alms of those who were entering the temple. When he saw Peter and John about to go into the temple, he began asking to receive alms. But Peter, along with John, fixed his gaze on him and said, "Look at us!" And he began to give them his attention, expecting to receive something from them. But Peter said, "I do not possess silver and gold, but what I do have I give to you: In the name of Jesus Christ the Nazarene—walk!"

And seizing him by the right hand, he raised him up; and immediately his feet and his ankles were strengthened. With a leap he stood upright and began to walk; and he entered the temple with them, walking and leaping and praising God. And all the people saw him walking and praising God; and they were taking note of him as being the one who used to sit at the Beautiful Gate of the temple to beg alms, and they were filled with wonder and amazement at what had happened to him. While he was clinging to Peter and John, all the people ran together to them at the so-called portico of Solomon, full of amazement.

The One, Jesus Christ, is very different than the Buddha, Gautama Siddhartha, as shown by the evidences shown above, and not only in *words* but in deeds and authority also. Each one was showing you the way: one to Nirvana, and the other to have eternal life via the resurrection in which He Himself was resurrected. In Buddhism, you have to spend your time in meditation in order to suppress all your cravings, lusts, desires, wants, and needs, as well as perform good works to gain merit points to go higher in the Samsara cycle and to eventually escape it. Whereas, being a follower of Jesus, you immediately possess eternal life and will be resurrected.

What does accepting the sacrifice of Jesus on the cross do for you with regard to your craving, lusts for power and control, greed, suffering, etc.?

It does not mean that the followers of Jesus do not have cravings, lust, desires, greed, wants, and needs, but that it no longer has a stronghold nor will it imprison a believer, and that the believer is able to overcome it by *living in the spirit* and by commanding that those cravings, lusts, desire, greed, wants, and needs go and leave him or her alone. On the spiritual side, the biblical scriptures instruct you to "Submit to God and resist the devil and he will flee from you" as in *James 4:7*. And in *Ephesians 6:13*, it says, "Therefore, take up the full armour of God, so that you will be able to resist in the evil day, and having done everything to stand firm." So the believer in Jesus has been given the tools and instructions to overcome all the cravings and sufferings.

32

How Can I Have Eternal Life Right Away and Not Get Stuck in the *Samsara Cycle?

Repenting, Confessing, and Receiving

A. Repentance from Your Sins

Matthew 4:17 says, "From that time Jesus began to preach and say, 'Repent, for the kingdom of heaven is at hand.'"

Luke 13:5 says, "I tell you, no, but unless you repent, you will all likewise perish."

B. Confession

Romans 10:8–10 says, "But what does it say? '*The word is near you,* in your mouth and in your heart,' that is, the word of faith which we are preaching, that if you confess with your mouth Jesus as Lord, and believe in your heart that God raised Him from the dead, you will be saved; for with the heart a person believes, resulting in righteousness, and with the mouth he confesses, resulting in salvation."

C. Receiving of the Holy Spirit

Acts 2:38 (~AD 30–74) Peter said to them, "Repent, and each of you be baptized in the name of Jesus Christ for the forgiveness of your sins, and you will receive the gift of the Holy Spirit."

Acts 8:14–17 says, "Now when the apostles in Jerusalem heard that Samaria had received the word of God, they sent them Peter and John, who came down and prayed for them that they might receive the Holy Spirit. For He had not yet fallen upon any of them; they had simply been baptized in the name of the Lord Jesus. Then they began laying their hands on them, and they were receiving the Holy Spirit."

33

Gautama Siddhartha (Buddha) and the Man on the Cross

When it comes to a personal belief, a person is free to believe whatever he or she chooses, even to believe that *pigs can fly*. There can be no coercion that everyone must believe in the same doctrine. In this comparative work, laying all things aside, regardless of doctrine and practices, it really boils down to the person of Gautama Siddhartha and the *man on the cross* and who they really are and had done. Then does what they were and what they had done testify to what they had said?

You need to consider and compare all that Gautama Siddhartha had done with what Jesus Christ had done (prophesied by the prophets of old, fulfilled and as testified by His witnesses). Gautama Siddhartha sat under a tree and meditated and claimed he had achieved complete enlightenment, and thus escaped the Samsara cycle and was in Nirvana. Jesus Christ was born on earth as a fulfilment to several prophecies by ancient prophets hundreds of years before His coming, healing the people suffering from blindness, was lame, had leprosy; raising the dead; feeding five thousand people with two loaves and five fishes with a leftover of twelve baskets full; casting out demons; walked on water; and rebuking and stilling the storm, etc., by the authority of His Words because of who He is—the Begotten Son of God the Father—and because He loves you. Jesus gave His life (crucified and died on the cross) for the sins of the world that He may save you and set you free from sin. He resurrected having victory over sin and death so that you too can be free of sin and receive eternal life. So great is His work and so great a salvation for those who are ready to accept Him.

Gautama Siddhartha, the Buddha, had never promised you eternal life nor guaranteed a trip to Nirvana but that you had to work your way, which may take years, to reach Nirvana. So great and compelling are the evidence set before you, not of fairy tales, gossips, or superstitions but the actual person of the Lord Jesus Christ, His power, authority, and command of His Words challenge a person to re-evaluate his or her standing in life because it has such drastic and significant impact on this life and the life after.

The list witnesses and testifies to the reality of Jesus Christ, the Begotten Son of God, who was born of a virgin, crucified, buried, and resurrected. His twelve apostles and the four who wrote the gospels: Matthew, Mark, Luke, and John, and then there is Peter, who was one of the twelve apostles, as well as James, the half-brother of Jesus. So write Peter and John these words:

In 1 John 1:1–4 (~AD 30–90), it says,

> What was from the beginning, what *we have heard, what we have seen with our eyes, what we have looked at and touched with our hands, concerning the Word of Life (Jesus Christ)—and the life was manifested, and we have seen and testify and proclaim to you the eternal life,* which was with the Father and was manifested to us—what we have seen and heard we proclaim to you also, so that you too may have fellowship with us; and indeed our fellowship is with the Father, and with His Son Jesus Christ. These things we write, so that our joy may be made complete.

In 2 Peter 1:16–17 (~AD 67), it says,

> For we did not follow cleverly devised tales when we made known to you the power and

coming of our Lord Jesus Christ, but *we were eyewitnesses of His majesty.* For when He received honour and glory from God the Father, such an utterance as this was made to Him by the Majestic Glory, "This is My beloved Son with whom I am well-pleased"—and we ourselves heard this utterance made from heaven when we were with Him on the holy mountain.

After the Resurrection:
John 20:25–29 says,

> So the other disciples were saying to him, "We have seen the Lord!" But he said to them, "Unless I see in His hands the imprint of the nails, and put my finger into the place of the nails, and put my hand into His side, I will not believe." After eight days His disciples were again inside, and Thomas (one of the twelve apostles) with them. Jesus came, the doors having been shut, and stood in their midst and said, "Peace be with you." Then He said to Thomas, "Reach here with your finger, and see My hands; and reach here your hand and put it into My side; and do not be unbelieving, but believing." *Thomas answered and said to Him, "My Lord and my God!"* Jesus said to him, "Because you have seen Me, have you believed? Blessed are they who did not see, and yet believed."

Acts 1:1–11 says,

> The first account I composed, Theophilus, about all that Jesus began to do and teach, until the day when He was taken up to heaven, after He had by the Holy Spirit given orders to the

171

apostles whom He had chosen. To these He also presented Himself alive after His suffering, by many convincing proofs, appearing to them over a period of forty days and speaking of the things concerning the kingdom of God. Gathering them together, He commanded them not to leave Jerusalem, but to wait for what the Father had promised, "Which," He said, "you heard of from Me; for John baptized with water, but you will be baptized with the Holy Spirit not many days from now." So when they had come together, they were asking Him, saying, "Lord, is it at this time You are restoring the kingdom to Israel?" He said to them, "It is not for you to know times or epochs which the Father has fixed by His own authority; but you will receive power when the Holy Spirit has come upon you; and you shall be My witnesses both in Jerusalem, and in all Judea and Samaria, and even to the remotest part of the earth." And after He had said these things, *He was lifted up while they were looking on, and a cloud received Him out of their sight. And as they were gazing intently into the sky while He was going, behold, two men in white clothing stood beside them. They also said, "Men of Galilee, why do you stand looking into the sky? This Jesus, who has been taken up from you into heaven, will come in just the same way as you have watched Him go into heaven."*

34

Life-Changing Action

Not only did Jesus have the power and authority to heal diseases, cast out demon, and raise the dead, but that He gave the same power to his disciples to do the same and even greater things. And is true even to this very day. Here are some of the examples recorded in the New Testament of the Bible:

Matthew 10:1 says, "Jesus summoned His twelve disciples and gave them authority over unclean spirits, to cast them out, and to heal every kind of disease and every kind of sickness."

Matthew 10:7–14 says,

> And as you go, preach, saying, "The kingdom of heaven is at hand." *Heal the sick, raise the dead, cleanse the lepers, cast out demons. Freely you received, freely give. Do not acquire gold, or silver, or copper for your money belts, or a bag for your journey, or even two coats, or sandals, or a staff; for the worker is worthy of his support.* And whatever city or village you enter, inquire who is worthy in it, and stay at his house until you leave that city. As you enter the house, give it your greeting. If the house is worthy, give it your blessing of peace. But if it is not worthy, take back your blessing of peace. Whoever does not receive you, nor heed

your words, as you go out of that house or that city, shake the dust off your feet.

A. Healing the Sick

Acts 3:1–16 says,

> Now Peter and John were going up to the temple at the ninth hour, the hour of prayer. And a man who had been lame from his mother's womb was being carried along, whom they used to set down every day at the gate of the temple, which is called Beautiful, in order to beg alms of those who were entering the temple. When he saw Peter and John about to go into the temple, he began asking to receive alms. But Peter, along with John, fixed his gaze on him and said, "Look at us!" And he began to give them his attention, expecting to receive something from them. But Peter said, "I do not possess silver and gold, but what I do have I give to you: In the name of Jesus Christ the Nazarene—walk!" And seizing him by the right hand, he raised him up; and immediately his feet and his ankles were strengthened. With a leap he stood upright and began to walk; and he entered the temple with them, walking and leaping and praising God. And all the people saw him walking and praising God; and they were taking note of him as being the one who used to sit at the Beautiful Gate of the temple to beg alms, and they were filled with wonder and amazement at what had happened to him. While he was clinging to Peter and John, all the people ran together to them at the so-called portico of Solomon, full of amazement. But when Peter saw this, he replied to the people, "Men of Israel,

why are you amazed at this, or why do you gaze at us, as if by our own power or piety we had made him walk? The God of Abraham, Isaac and Jacob, the God of our fathers, has glorified His servant Jesus, the one whom you delivered and disowned in the presence of Pilate, when he had decided to release Him. But you disowned the Holy and Righteous One and asked for a murderer to be granted to you, but put to death the Prince of life, the one whom God raised from the dead, a fact to which we are witnesses. And on the basis of faith in His name, it is the name of Jesus, which has strengthened this man whom you see and know; and the faith, which comes through Him has given him this perfect health in the presence of you all."

B. Raising the Dead

Acts 9:36–41 says,

> Now in Joppa there was a disciple named Tabitha (which translated in Greek is called Dorcas); this woman was abounding with deeds of kindness and charity which she continually did. And it happened at that time that she fell sick and died; and when they had washed her body, they laid it in an upper room. Since Lydda was near Joppa, the disciples, having heard that Peter was there, sent two men to him, imploring him, "Do not delay in coming to us." So Peter arose and went with them. When he arrived, they brought him into the upper room; and all the widows stood beside him, weeping and showing all the tunics and garments that Dorcas used to make while she was with them. But Peter sent

them all out and knelt down and prayed, and turning to the body, he said, "Tabitha, arise." And she opened her eyes, and when she saw Peter, she sat up. And he gave her his hand and raised her up; and calling the saints and widows, he presented her alive. It became known all over Joppa, and many believed in the Lord.

From the above examples, we can see that not only did Jesus have the authority and power over death, demons, and diseases, but that He was able to commission or give power and authority for His followers to do the same. The same cannot be said of Gautama Siddhartha, the Buddha, or his followers.

Further to that, the disciples of Jesus would not surrender what those that had touched with their hand, seen with their eyes, heard with their ears the reality of the Lord Jesus Christ, and they all died for their testimony!

Simon Peter died on the cross.

Andrew, brother of Simon Peter, died being scourged and tortured. James, the son of Zebedee, died by the sword.

John, also the son of Zebedee, died in exile on the island of Patmos.

Bartholomew was tortured to death.

Matthew, killed by the sword.

Thomas died by the spear.

James, the son of Alphaeus, was beaten and stoned to death.

Thaddaeus was crucified in AD 72.

Simon the Zealot was crucified in AD 74.

Paul was beheaded in Rome in AD 66.

35

Ancient Sacred Vedic Sacred Hindu Texts References

Table of Contents

C. Self-Realization (Buddhist's term for Enlightenment) and Possession
   (i)   Introduction
   (ii)   Purpose of Life
   (iii) Entrance into the body by the "Self" or "Atman"
   (iv)   The Mantram as a weapon to destroy the self-will.
   (v)   The prana (energy or Atman ("Self") exiting the body.
   (vi)   Union with an Eternal Being
   (vii) Detachment of Oneself in order to achieve the Self, Atman or Self-Realization
   (viii) The "Self" or Atman is immortal and Immeasurable
   (ix)   The "Self"
   (x)   Union with Krishna, Vishnu, the Self, Atman
   (xi)   When Krishna enters a person
   (xii) Self-Realization and Possession
   (xiii) Self-Realization and Dis-possession

D. Self-Realization and Freedom from Attachments
   (i)   Attainment of the perfect yoga
   (ii)   Attainment of Freedom from all attachments
   (iii) Krishna the Divine Self
   (iv)   Complete control by Krishna
   (v)   Dualities of Life
   (vi)   Spiritual Wisdom in the Divine Self or Krishna
   (vii) Two Paths to Self-Realization
   (viii) Surrendering to the Divine Self or Krishna
   (ix)   Knowledge of the Divine Self or Krishna
   (x)   United mind with the Divine Self or Brahman
   (xi)   Freedom from Old Age and Death
   (xii) Benefits of total devotion to Krishna

E. Self-Realization and Renunciation
   (i)   Introduction
   (ii)   Two kinds of Renunciation
   (iii) Freedom to Kill
   (iv)   Mastering Renunciation

I. Self-Realization and Yoga Mantram
 (i) Definition of OM (or AUM), TAT and SAT
 (ii) Priestly Chants
 (iii) Repeated Chants in the Vedas
 (iv) Significance of A U M

NB: The following documentation of Hindu doctrines are from my book entitled *Hinduism and the Man on the Cross*.

Hindu Doctrines from the following Sacred Vedic Hindu Texts:

(i) Bhagavad Gita and the major Upanishads as translated by Mr. Eknath Easwaran,
(ii) The major Puranas as translated by the Dharmic Scripture Team of India, October 2002.
(iii) The Mahbharata as translated by Mr. Ramesh Menon.

A. Samsara Cycle

(i) Introduction

Samsara is the doctrine of continual rebirths, whereby a person reaches higher and higher in the "Wheel of Life" until he or she achieves immortality, enlightenment, illumination or in Union with the Atman or Universal Soul or Spirit. Conversely, a person can go lower and lower into the wheel of life and devolve into the lower hierarchy or lower forms of life. Where one returns to in the rebirth depends on the merits or demerits earned in this life. One can get stuck in the Samsara cycle for hundreds or thousands of lifetime if one does not attain immortality, and that is with the assumption that one is sent back to suffer the misery and depravation of life. While stuck in the Samsara cycle, a person can be sent to so-called hell temporarily to pay for the demerits or to the homes of the gods or devalokas to temporarily enjoy the merits earned and after which the person will be returned to earth to try again. The underlying philosophy is that a person gets many chances at life and that you may be living next to previous folks who are mass murderers, rapist, etc., like Joseph Stalin, Adolf Hitler, or Gen. Pol Pot. Or have them marrying you in this new life or marry your daughters. And also, it is not as severe a crime to kill someone as he or she will be reborn again. A person will never know if he or she had earned sufficient merits to overcome his demerits and is therefore never certain if he or she will go to the devaloka when he or she dies.

(ii) The Cycle of Life

Men are reborn again and again but have no knowledge of their past life because they have no access to such knowledge, even Arjuna, the son of Indra. Krishna elected to be reborn several times for the welfare of the world. (*Bhagavad Git, chapter 4, Wisdom in Action*)

Comments: The fact that Krishna is reborn again and again tells you that he had not attained immortality but stuck in the Samsara cycle, and yet he is regarded as a major deity, an Avatar of Vishnu and immortal.

(iii) All creatures must go through the Cycle of Life

(iii.a) Krishna tells that at the end of the age, all creatures returned to unmanifested matter, and he will send them forth again at the beginning of the new cycle. (*Bhagavad Gita, chapter 9, The Royal Path*)

Comments: If all things and life will be recycled, then what is the point of doing anything, as all things come to nothing and is then recycled?

(iii.b) Krishna's Secret Knowledge and the Samara Cycle

Krishna shared the secret of how to acquire "knowledge" or jnana and "life force" or vijnana so that a person can be free from all evil, and this great knowledge is a great purifier. It is righteous and imperishable and joyful to practice and experience. And those without faith in the supreme law of life cannot attain Krishna but return to the life of continuous rebirths or from death to death. (*Bhagavad Gita, chapter 9, The Royal Path*)

Comments: Knowledge did not set Krishna free from evil because he intentionally perjured himself as in section N (i), and to lie is evil! To intentionally lie is to know the truth, but elected to lie in order to achieve a certain gain, control or advantage! So how can good come from evil? There have been no proofs of rebirths

(iv) Krishna is Everything

After many rebirths, rare are the people who seek refuge in Krishna and **see Krishna in everything**. Many elect to follow their own nature and worship **lower gods.** *(Bhagavad Gita, chapter 7, Wisdom & Realization)*

Comments: Here, the Bhagavad Gita is saying that there are lower and higher gods, meaning that there are many gods with different rankings. I wonder how the gods are ranked? Do they carry a special sign so we can know the difference, or do they have signs in their forehead so we know their ranks? Who has the higher rank than Krishna or Vishnu, Shiva and Brahma? Do you know among those mentioned who is the highest-rank as that we do not waste our time with lower-ranked gods? What happens when the highest ranking of the gods has moral failures such as sinning by lying or being deceitful or lustful?

(v) Krishna is responsible for Rebirths

(v.a) Krishna claimed that it is he who decides and arranges for people their rebirths again and again. Lust, anger, and greed are the three doors to hell, and a person must avoid it at any cost. *(Bhagavad Gita, chapter 16, Two Paths)*

Comments: Krishna (i) raged (ii) perjured himself, entered into conflict with Agni (fire god) and Arjuna (Indra's son), (iii) entered into conflict with Indra, and (iv) entered into conflict with Shiva in the Mahabharata stories. From the examples given, Krishna should send himself and including Indra, Shiva, and Brahma for retraining or reeducation and be reborn into lower hierarchy of evolution, but it seems that they continued to be worshipped today!

It is surprising to read that Krishna did not include killing and lying, as the other two items are evil. But then Krishna intentionally perjured himself, so why should he not be sent to rebirths? And if that is Krishna's responsibilities, then he would have sent Brahma, Indra, and Shiva to rebirths for their guilt of lusts as shown in this section (x). And if Krishna had sent them to rebirths, how is Brahma and Vishnu going to be able to worship Shiva and his penis as found in *(a) Shiva Maha Purana 5.1 Vidyeshwar Samhita 5.1.15 Worshipping the Idol of Shiva, (b) Shiva Maha Purana 5.2 Shiva Samhita 5.2.13 The Methods of Worshipping Shiva.* So who runs and operates the Samsara cycle when Krishna was preoccupied with the Arjuna in the

Kurukshetra War in the Indus Valley? And there is nowhere to be found that says Krishna is omnipresent. Dang! The Samsara cycle must have taken leave of its operation for a short while.

(v.b) It is I, Krishna, who assigned those who are demonic to rebirth after rebirth or death after death, the demonic to wombs with similar characteristics, and they degrade and fall lower and lower still. (*Bhagavad Gita, chapter 16, Two Paths*)

Comments: It does seem that the term *demonic* is assigned to behaviour instead of an entity. And that anyone can be demonic if his or her behaviour did not conform to that of the devotees and are assigned to constant deaths and rebirths. Therefore, for you and I, we are designed for rebirths and therefore classified as demonic. Here Krishna claimed that he is the one who is the authority of the Samsara cycle and designs who gets to be reborn and who attains immortality. So then the question becomes who then is the authority when Krishna died in the Mahabharata, and who operates the Samsara cycle when Krishna is away in accompanying Arjuna in battle?

Furthermore, if one of the person had descended farther and farther or degraded down the evolutionary ladder, let's say, amoebae, how are the amoebas able to earn merits again to ascend up the evolutionary ladder? Or let us say if a person is degraded down to a monkey or ape, how is that ape or monkey able to work his way up and be human again? In this instance, Krishna claimed to be the judge and executioner, and how is he going to judge himself as a liar? Will he send himself for rebirth as a monkey or amoebae? So there is a real possibility that some of the dogs, cats, or even rats in your neighbourhood in India are your close relatives or parents? In section D (iii), Krishna is described as a demon and has a look of demons, so how is Krishna going to send himself to hell?

(vi) Krishna teaches on how to be free from the Rebirth Cycle.

Krishna speaks of nature as near and yet so far, and that in the cosmos, ego and intellect are five senses of the body and five senses of the mind, and the five senses considered are pleasure and pain, desire and revulsion, the entire being, intelligence and will. All these are knowledge: humility, honesty, nonviolence, patience, self-depreciation, and the perception at birth, death, old age, illness and pain are evil, detachment, no dependence on wife, children or home, same attitude toward pain or pleasure, total devotion to Krishna, solitary life, and the continual dedication to yoga. In order to reach the Brahman, he is totally unattached to anything and yet support the universe, has no beginning or end, is transcendental, eternal, is beyond what is and what is not, is totally free of the gunas (sattvas, rajas, and tamas), he is within every creature and beyond, subtle, beyond the grasp of the mind (the idea or concept of duality).

Attachments cause the soul to give birth to good and evil, and regardless of how a man lives, if he experiences the **Brahman, he is free from the Samsara cycle of rebirths.**

The three ways to realize the universal soul or spirit is by (a) dhyana (yogic meditation), (b) gunas (ability to control the sattvas, rajas, and tamas), and (c) karma (Hindu universal law of action and reaction), and the ignorance of these three ways lead to worship. And they too must cross the sea of death and get reborn. A person will only see god, if he sees god in everything and is deathless in this mortal world. When a man sees the actions in the world by the gunas and never the soul or the atman, he then truly sees the soul is without action. The Brahman is without beginning and lives in every being and does not act, not in touch by action; therefore, it is untainted and immaculate. A person who can differentiate the difference between the body and the knower of the eternal soul or atman becomes free and receive liberation or is fully illuminated or realized. (*Mahabharata vol. 2, book 6 Bheeshma Parva, 7 The Bhagavad Gita*)

Comments: Even though Krishna was able to point out about human nature, even before the dawn of western psychology, he preached the doctrine of the Samsara cycle of continual deaths and rebirths, and the concept of man achieving immortality so that he can be "as god," which cannot be proven and is the oldest trick of the ages. But then it comes from the master of deception and illusion, and therefore you cannot know when and if he is telling the truth or a lie because his preaching usually has both truth and lie all intertwined! The concept of the Samsara cycle is derived from the fact that the snake sheds its skin and is "continually reborn." Krishna can claim all that he wanted, but does it have any validity since he had proven himself with his own words that he is a liar and deceiver? A person is not a liar because he lies but that he lies because he is a liar. It is a subtle difference but a very important and crucial one. A person must be consistent with his words and claims, and how much more so if he is a godhead or deity.

A DECEIVER cannot be righteous or holy because the moment he lies, he becomes unclean as he is tainted by sin. Krishna willingly perjured himself because he was unable the resolve the matter without doing so, as in Mahabharata vol. 2, book 7 Droan Parva, 12 Arjuna's Dream p. 323. But Krishna cannot perjure himself if it is not "in" him or his nature. He is only showing his true nature, a DECEIVER and a PERJURER. This is a dangerous doctrine in that if a deity that is highly esteemed by his millions of devotees is a deceiver and liar, it affects the devotees mentally and psychologically, in that it is acceptable for a god to lie or deceive, then there should be no problem or difficulty for the devotees to do likewise. You begin to wonder if this behaviour becomes deeply imbedded or ingrained in the Hindu psyche.

(vii) Krishna pronounced he is free of all Karmas

God made men with his own nature and dharma, and by following his nature, he will prosper from his desire, and by following his dharma, he worships gods, and the gods in turn will nurture him. Being unattached to all desires, lust, rage, fear, and evil a man achieves eternal bliss. Rage and lust are deadly enemies, and the deluded intellect feeds on them. In order to go past both lust and rage, one must transcend the intellect as it is the atman that sets one free. **Krishna pronounced that he is free of all karma and yet owned everything.** (*Mahabharata vol. 2 book 6: Bheeshma Parva, 4 Bhagavad Gita*)

(viii) Krishna and the Samsara Cycle

The field is made up of the body, which includes the mind, and it is made up of the nature and its inherent energy and its ego and self-will. Krishna is the knower, which is hidden in the field and is the true divine self. The body and the mind are all part of the nature and its inherent energy. The true self is the knower and the pure. The soul can never be lost because all are partakers of the eternal nature of the Purusha, even as it goes through countless **cycles of rebirths** but will in the need rest in the eternal spirit of Krishna. *(Bhagavad Gita, chapter 13, The Field & the Knower)*

Comments: Krishna claimed he is the knower, but he also claimed many, many things and that includes being the lord maya or illusion, deception, and lies. So how are you going to trust Krishna?

(ix) Devotees who are liberated from all attachment will live with Krishna in his heavenly home.

Krishna is not only the Atman (universal soul) but transcends the Atman. The liberated self, now an immortal soul, is in union with Krishna but does not become Krishna. Those in union will live with Krishna in his loka (heavenly abode). (Bhagavad Gita, chapter 15, The Supreme Self)

Comments: One would assume that if you worship Krishna, you would live with him and his 16,108 wives in his heavenly home. Now what will happen to your wife is your wife's not coming to the heavenly home at the same time, and you are left to your lonely self. If your earthly wife is reborn, she may not marry you at all in your next life because she has more or less merits than you're reborn to a different time and or status, and to make it worse, she possible married someone else better than you. Or is there a possibility that there will be shared wives or husbands in the heaven places. The Mahabharata has no difficulty with one woman having five husbands! Furthermore, how is Krishna, who is without attachments, desire, or emotion, to love any of his wives? The only way he can treat any of his wives is that they become just inanimate objects.

(x) Vedic practitioners will go to heaven but will be reborn again

Those who conducted ritual sacrifices drink the Soma and free themselves of evil and will go to heaven, where the gods are, and enjoy their celestial pleasures, but when their merits are used up, there are reborn into this world of endless death. Only those who meditate and worship me constantly and without attachments, **I, Krishna will supply all their needs.** (*Bhagavad Gita, chapter 9, The Royal Path*)

Comments: If the Hindu gods can have sex and several consorts, will Krishna also supply consorts to all the vedic practitioners in the celestial abodes? You can imagine those Vedic practitioners who are handicapped were unable to earn more merits and are therefore deigned for a shorter time in their heavens. But, nevertheless, all are deigned to endless births and deaths. Krishna was never a Vedic deity, so then how is it possible for the Vedic believers to worship Krishna? Where will the billions of righteous people, who are not Hindus, in the world go to when they die, and is it Krishna who will judge them? And if not, Krishna is totally useless to nonbelievers, who are not Hindus! And if yes, how is it fair to worship someone whom you do not know and who is a deceiver or liar? In practical terms, the Hindus in India worship more than just Krishna but pantheons of other gods and goddesses because he is unable to deliver all their needs.

(xi) The Soul and Rebirths

The soul can never be lost because all are partaker of the eternal nature of the Purusha, even as it goes through countless cycles of rebirths but will in need of rest in the eternal spirit of Krishna. (*Bhagavad Gita, chapter 13, The Field & the Knower*)

Comments: Just because Krishna said it, it does not mean that it is true as Krishna had been known to perjure himself intentionally as in the Mahabharata V2, book 7 Droan Parva, 12 Arjuna's Dream p. 323.

B. Krishna's Doctrine: Dharma

(i) The law of dharma, which is action or deed, is you reap what you sow. (*Bhagavad Gita chapter 3, Selfless Service*)

Comments: This law of dharma is not totally true unless there is a final judgment day for all. In Krishna's doctrine of the Samsara cycle or continual rebirth, depending on the amount of accumulated merits, a person will either go up the ladder or devolve. Adolf Hitler, after killing more than six million people, will eventually work his way up the ladder of the Samsara cycle and finally to be at one with Krishna!

(ii) Eight Paths of the Dharma

The gods do not protect men with their weapons, and for those who wish success he blesses with intelligence and he would know the eight **paths of the dharma (religious and moral law): sacrifice, study, asceticism, charity, truth, mercy, forgiveness, and contentment.** And the first four exist from vanity, and the last four are found in a truly great man. As fire purifies gold, so does a man by his character, honesty by his conduct, and courage when in panic. Poverty tests a man to have self-control and friends in time of danger and trials. The question is how does Krishna fare with the moral law of truth when he claimed that he is the master deceiver or liar? (*Mahabharata vol. 2, book 5 Udyoga Parva 7 A Blind King's Terror*)

Comments: Both Krishna and Shiva interfered by siding with Arjuna in the Kurukshetra War, so it is very difficult to take this eight paths of the doctrine seriously because when Krishna, Shiva, Brahma, and Vishnu all fought, quarrel among themselves, and all are deceivers or liars, how can one possibly trust anything said? Would you trust your very good friend or spouse if he or she is a known liar or deceiver? The character must conform to the word or the word cannot be trusted nor the speaker. Poverty does not test a person as much as that of a rich person.

(iii) Vedic Practitioners will be stuck in the Samsara Cycle

(iii.a) Those who practice ritual and sacrifices as instructed in the Vedas will never reach their goal of immortality and achieve union with the supreme self, Krishna. After death, they will enjoy heaven for a time, and after their merits are used up, they are reborn again and again to have another chance to renounce their attachments and desires. (*Bhagavad Gita, chapter 9, The Royal Path*)

Comments: Here the doctrine is that a person after he or she dies goes to "heaven" and enjoy the merits won, and after it is used up, they get kicked out of heaven and back down to earth through rebirths. So that their residency in heaven is only temporary. Therefore, in this instance, the husband and wife can easily be separated and never shall they meet, as they had different level or merits. It also means that all thousands devoted Vedic priest for over hundreds of years, with their sacrifices and meditations, were stuck in the Samsara cycle and were reborn into the miseries of life.

(iii.b) Those who conducted ritual, sacrifices, drink the Soma, and free themselves of evil will go to heaven, where the gods are, and enjoy their celestial pleasures, but when their merits are used up, they are reborn into this world of endless death. Only those who meditate and worship me constantly and without attachments, I, Krishna will supply all their needs. (*Bhagavad Gita, chapter 9, The Royal Path*)

Comments: This statement, in reality, is actually very contradictory because why would Krishna supply all their needs because when illumined, they will have no feeling, needs, or wants or any attachments.

(iii.c) Those who practice ritual and sacrifices as instructed in the Vedas will never reach their goal of immortality and achieve union with the supreme self, Krishna. After death, they will enjoy heaven for a time, and when their merits are used up, they are reborn again and again to have another chance to renounce their attachments and desires. (*Bhagavad Gita, chapter 9, The Royal Path*)

Comments: Those who did not earn sufficient merit are devolved into beasts, and even worse, when they can possibly be devolved into viruses and bacteria, and how then is it possible to earn sufficient merits to return as humans again? Do the bacterias and viruses earn their merits by the number of humans they infect?

(iv) Self-realization is greater than Vedic practices

(iv.a) Knowledge is twofold: higher and lower. The study of the Vedas, linguistics, rituals, and all the arts can be called "lower knowledge." The higher is that which leads to self-realization. **The rituals and the sacrifices described in the Vedas deal with lower**

knowledge. The sages ignored these rituals and went in search of higher knowledge. Such rituals are unsafe rafts for crossing the sea of Samsara, of birth and death. Doomed to shipwreck who tried to cross the sea of Samsara on the poor rafts. Ignorant of their ignorance, yet wise in their own esteem, these deluded men. Proud of their vain learnings go round and round, like the blind led by the blind. Living in darkness, immature, unaware of any higher good or goal, they fall again and again into the sea. But those who are pure in heart, who practice meditation and conquer their senses and passions, shall attain the Immortal Self, source of all light and source of all life. Action prompted by pleasure or profit cannot help anyone cross the sea. Seek a teacher, who has self-realized the self, to the student whose heart is full of love, who has conquered his senses and passion, the teacher will reveal the Lord of Love. (*The Mandaka Upanishad. Part 1*)

Comments: Here, the Mandaka Upanishad reinforced the allegations that the Vedic practices are inferior to self-realization or illumination, where a devotee can achieve immortality. If Krishna, Indra, Shiva, or even Brahma are unable to control their desire to deceive and lie or perjure themselves, what chance do you think you have to achieve immortality? If the Hindu gods themselves do not make good examples, what hope is there for us mere humans? The only hope is as found in the biblical doctrine, where God provides for himself a lamb (Jesus Christ) of sacrifice for sin so that it fulfils all the conditions to be free from sins, the curse of the law and death.

(iv.b) Those who practice ritual and sacrifices as instructed in the Vedas will never reach their goal of immortality and achieve union with the supreme self, Krishna. After death, they will enjoy heaven for a time, and when their merits are used up, they are reborn again and again to have another chance to renounce their attachments and desires. (*Bhagavad Gita, chapter 9, The Royal Path*)

Comments: The Age of the Vedas had passed as the believer and devotees became attracted to the idea of achieving immortality, and to do that is to become one as gods. This idea of achieving immortality became the forefront of Hindu thought, religious philosophy and doctrine, and it is then labelled as self-realization. The only path to immortality is to be at one with the godhead or labelled "Universal Spirit," "Universal Soul," or Atman, Indra, Krishna, the Spirit of Brahma or Vishnu. Self-realization is not coming to know your personal "self" but that of god or the Universal Spirit in you. The god, "Universal Spirit," or Universal Atman is in reality a foreign entity or Spirit, and you only find that in the sacred Hindu text, and that is as shown below. The foreign Spirit will enter you after all the barriers are deconstructed or destroyed and will leave you when you die and that is also shown below. In religious terms, it is called "spiritual possession."

Knowledge can be described as inferior knowledge because its practice did not lead to immortality and be at one with the godhead, Atman, Universal Spirit or the self but is stuck in continual rebirths and deaths. The practices of the Vedas welcome the deities to the sacrifice and worship whereby the devotees asked for protection, wealth, prosperity, power, and progenies but there never was a promise of being at one with the deity, thus attaining immortality.

The Vedas are described as lower. Here lies a very misleading doctrine as the "self" or your "Universal Self or Atman" is not about you or soul or your spirit, but it is in reality an external reality or spirit that will come into you and take over, and becoming your new person, thus, is termed a realizing the SELF or becoming aware of the SELF. You will see in the sacred texts quoted that the self will come and enter into you when you make yourself ready and leave you when you die. So when you prepare yourself through meditation or yogic meditation, the SELF will enter you and thus you realized the SELF, thus the term self-realization. That is called possession by alien entity. All this is done under the pretext of unity with the self, thus attaining immortality.

The attraction and temptation is that an ordinary person can be as god. So all Brahmins and Gurus who practiced the art of meditation to free themselves of all attachments, truly prepared themselves to be filled with Spirit of the Self, and you can call it Brahma, Krishna, or Vishnu, but the result is the same. Unity with the Brahma, Krishna, or Vishnu and become one with him and therefore be as or like god. Thus fulfilling the scriptures in the Bible (Genesis chapter 3:1–5), when Satan (embodied as a Serpent) tempted Eve in the Garden of Eden,

> Now the serpent was more crafty than any beast of the field which the LORD God had made. And he said to the woman, "Indeed, has God said, 'You shall not eat from any tree of the garden'?" The woman said to the serpent, "From the fruit of the trees of the garden we may eat; but from the fruit of the tree which is in the middle of the garden, God has said, 'You shall not eat from it or touch it, or you will die.'" The serpent said to the woman, "You surely will not die! For God knows that in the day you eat from it your eyes will be opened, and **you will be like or as God**, knowing good and evil."

C. Self-Realization (Buddhist's term for Enlightenment) and Possession

(i) Introduction

When your free will or self-will is destroyed, then you lose the ability to think or decide for yourself. You essentially surrender it to a foreign entity or spirit that enters into you, and that is defined as possession. That is exactly what the sacred Hindu texts tell you what happened, and it is as shown below. The purpose of it all is to be in "union" with the foreign spirit or so-called divine spirit and therefore be as one with god. That is the ultimate goal of self-realization: free of attachment, renunciation, illumination, yogic meditation, etc.; that is, to be one with the Atman or Universal Soul or Spirit.

(ii) The purpose of Life

The purpose of life is to attain self-realization or union with the divine Krishna, or they will be stuck in the Samsara cycle of rebirth. *(Bhagavad Gita, chapter 9, The Royal Path)*

Comments: In their rebirths, they either go up the ladder of life or they devolve into lower beings. Here lies the threat for the general populace in that they are stuck in the misery of this life, and this doctrine gives them, they think, a way out of poverty and the caste system. But it is another lie because Krishna informs you himself that he is the master of the Maya or Illusion, a great Deceiver.

(iii) Entrance into the body by the "Self" or Atman
The Self thought, "How can this be without me?
If speaking is done by speech, breathing by
Breath, seeing by eyes, hearing by ears, smelling
By nose, and meditation by the mind,
Then who am I?" **Entering the body
Through the gateway at the crown of the head.
He passed into the three states of consciousness
in which the Self resides.**
Filled with wonder, we sing: "I see the Lord."
So his name is Idamdra, "He who sees."
The name Indra stands for Idamdra.
The gods do like to sit behind a veil;
Indeed they like to sit behind a veil. (*Aitareya Upanishad Part 1:3:11–13*)
Comments: Please do not be misled as the word self here refers to the Universal Soul or Spirit, which is Krishna, Brahma or Vishnu, etc., and it is not you but a foreign entity. So when you forced the mind and body to renounce all things, you destroy your self-will. Here is the very core of Hindu meditation doctrine and tenet of the Hindu faith! Krishna claimed that he is Indra. The Indra is the god who disguised himself and raped Ahalya, wife of king Maharishi.

(iv) The Mantram as a weapon to destroy the self-will
He (Brahma) is the source of all the powers of life.
He is the Lord of all, **the great seer**
Who dwells forever in the cosmic womb.
May **he purify our consciousness.**
O Lord (Brahma) in whom alone we can find peace,

May we see **your divine Self and be freed**
From all impure thoughts and all fear.
O Lord, from whom we receive the mantram
As a weapon to destroy our self-will,
Reveal yourself, protector of all. *(The Shvetashvatara Upanishad)*

Comments: Same as in (i) above. The mantram is like a procla-
mation of welcome to the Universal Self or Spirit after your self-will
is destroyed, meaning that a person is unable to resist the possession
of his body! Herein lies the secret of Yogic meditation to destroy the
self-will of the meditator!

(v) The prana (energy or Atman, "Self") exiting the body.

The mind and thoughts are locked in the heart when the consciousness leaves through the nine gates. When life's vital energy
(prana) is withdrawn, the person has no access to his will. The prana
must be made to move to the head through meditation. Only the
yogi has control of the movements of the prana. **So if the prana exits
through the aperture of Brahma, there is no rebirth but union
with Brahma** or a state of Samadhi, thus achieving immortality. The
Bhagavad Gita quoted the Chandogya Upanishad VIII.6.5–6, "That
if the **prana goes upward to the crown of the head, going through
the aperture of Brahma,** he goes to eternal life but if it exits through
any gates, it will fail." Repeating the OM, mantram of the imperishable Brahman, which Krishna will lead you to union with eternal
Brahman. *(Bhagavad Gita, chapter 8, The Eternal Godhead p. 161)*

Comments: This is the text (i), the Aitareya Upanishad, and it
tells the partial truth about the purpose of the meditation and the
renunciation of all attachments so that the self, Atman or Universal
Soul or Spirit can enter the person and possess the person. The
Shvetashvatara Upanishad tells you that the **yogic meditation process with its mantram destroys the will of the person or protective
barriers** so that the Atman or Universal Self or Brahma can enter the
person. In the *Bhagavad Gita*, Krishna tells you that He is the Atman
or Universal Spirit. How much clearer do you want to hear of what
the meditation process is doing to a person under the false presence
of achieving self-realization?

When you see that the deities, Brahma, Vishnu, Shiva, Indra, etc. are all associated with or personification of the serpent, are all **DECEIVERS**, how can you possibly expect the truth because truths and deceptions do not lie in the same bed together. You are either one or the other. You can see for yourself that from the following summarized passages from the sacred Hindu texts on renunciation and self-realization. What it is really trying to do is to deceive you. All deceptions come with a bait or something that is good, something that is far and above your wildest dream, "to be at one with the deity" that you may attain the ultimate goal of immortality. No new doctrines from an external source is introduced here, but all of them can be found in the Hindu sacred texts. The truth is found in the sacred Hindu texts itself, and it is found in the details as to what being One with or be as god entails. In the *Bhagavad Gita*, the Eternal Godhead tells of the Spirit leaving through the Brahma aperture or opening, which is the crown of the head or the same way that it came into the person.

(vi) Union with an Eternal Being or Atman

(vi.a) It is not the postures or exercise (hatha yoga) but the union with the Eternal Being, Atman, through the practice of the discipline of the mind to detach from the dualities of life and achieve profound peace. *(Bhagavad Gita, chapter 2, Self-Realization)*

Comments: Same as in (iv) Once, it is detached, it no long has any control.

(vi.b) Once a person knows his true nature, he is in touch with his own immortality and realize his union with the eternal Being. *(Bhagavad Gita, chapter 2, Self-realization)*

Comments: Same as in (iii). Here in the union with the spirit. meaning is joined to the Universal Spirit or Atman. and it is the Atman that has the full control of the body. When that happens, a person lost all sense of feelings, wants, needs, desires, hunger, thirst. You can see the evidence of that in some of the Hindu festivals, like the Thaipusam festival, where the men pierced or skewed themselves with sharpened steel spikes and parade or boasts their condition to the general populace. How does Hinduism differentiate between being possessed by a god or a demon, especially when Krishna tells you himself that he is also a demon?

(vii) Detachment of oneself in order to achieve the Self, Atman or Self-Realization

Those who are able to detach themselves through yoga have come to fully realize the self, thus achieved self-realization, having full control of their sense instead of letting their sense controlling them. (*Bhagavad Gita, chapter 2, Self-Realization*)

Comments: Same as in (iii). Here is a contradictory statement in that the person does not have full control of his senses as he had already surrendered them, and with that, the Universal-Self, Krishna, Vishnu or Brahma that has full control, and that is why it is termed "spiritual possession," meaning your body is possessed by a foreign spirit or demon.

(viii) The "Self" or Atman is immortal and immeasurable

The impermanent has no reality, as reality lies in the eternal, and those who can distinguish the two has attained the end of all knowledge. The eternal is in the universal and is indestructible, unchanging, and imperishable. That which dwells in the mortal body is immortal and immeasurable. (*Bhagavad Gita, chapter 2, Self-Realization*)

Comments: Here the doctrine is teaching you that the Universal Spirit or Atman that had entered you is immortal and immeasurable, and therefore, you had attained or is in union with immortality, but that is only temporary as once you get dispossessed, you are back down to reality. So do you want Indra, a rapist, and Brahma, who lusted and lack self-control, or similarly Shiva to be the deity you worship? Krishna is both a deceiver and liar to inhabit your body. Instead of being free, you become possessed and not able to free yourself, and that is like being imprisoned for the rest of this earthly life. The temporary is also reality as it is deigned that mankind should live once and then die to face judgement before God, which no one can escape.

(ix) The Self

(viii.a) You are never born nor die, change or unchanged but unborn, **eternal, immutable, and continues on when the body dies, acquiring a new body.**

(viii.b) The self cannot be killed, hurt, burnt, nor affected as it is everlasting and infinite, and therefore unaffected by grief nor joy or sorrow nor pain.

(viii.c) Since the self is unchanging, immortal, eternal, affected by anything, then a warrior when confronted by war should be pleased, and to not fight the battle is sin, therefore violating your dharma.

(viii.d) Death means the attainment of heaven, and victory in war is enjoyment of the earth, and to engage in a great battle is to be free from sin. *(Bhagavad Gita, chapter 2, Self-realization)*

Comments: Right here, the doctrine tells you that when your body dies, the Atman, Universal Spirit or self will dispose you and acquire another body! So what happens to your immortality or being at one with the Atman or Universal Soul/Spirit or Krishna, etc.? You will find that the spirit is actually a supernatural entity, a member of the fallen angels or demons. The self, Atman or universal Spirit will be judged and be thrown into the lake of eternal fire found in the book of Revelations in the Christian Bible. It tells you that the battle with sin had been won, and there is no more continual battle with sin. When Jesus Christ was crucified and resurrected, sin had been severed and death defeated. For those who accepted the sacrifice of Jesus, the Son of God, and His resurrection, they will inherit eternal life. To inherit eternal life is not an earned reward but a free gift of God if you, by faith, accepted that His Son, Jesus Christ was crucified for your sin and was resurrected that you may have life everlasting.

(x) Union with Krishna, Vishnu, the Self, Atman

(x.a) The mystical union with Krishna (an Avatar of Vishnu) is possible through devotion, **when one sees Krishna (Vishnu) in every creature** and enters a state of divine love. *(Bhagavad Gita, chapter 4, Wisdom in Action)*

Comments: You cannot enter into a state of divine love because you have no feelings at all having renounced all such attachments like love, etc. And Krishna cannot love because if he is truly fully realized, he has no feelings at all. One big fat zero! You cannot reject all attachments and renounce everything and still have the feeling and action of love.

(x.b) If one can be totally devoted to Krishna alone, the purity of the will alone will free the person from his selfish motives and release him from his karma, and his spirit will be free to have union with Krishna. *(Bhagavad Gita, chapter 9, The Royal Path)*
Comments: Same as in (xiv). But then, Krishna admittedly is a master of illusions or Maya and is a self-declared deceiver, so you will be united with Krishna and be like him, a deceiver or liar!

(xi) When Krishna enters a person
Krishna, when entering every heart, gives the ability to remember and understand as well as to take it away. All scriptures lead to Krishna, and he is their author and wisdom. Krishna, who is beyond the changeless and changing, is the Supreme Lord that enters the cosmos and supports it from within. Krishna is the source of all wisdom, and those that see the self sees truly. *(Bhagavad Gita, chapter 15, The Supreme Self)*
Comments: This statement is contrary to that which states that Krishna is in everyone as claimed is true, then Krishna does not have to enter every heart as stated above. The fact that he had to enter implies that Krishna is an external entity and needed to enter a person, and that is true to the claim that the spirit enters the person through the crown of the head, as in *Aitareya Upanishad Part 1:3:11–13*. How can Krishna be wisdom when he perjured himself in that he knowingly lied and, therefore, committed evil! If there is nothing wrong with Krishna lying, then all his devotees should be able to follow his example and lie without any repercussions.

(xii) Self-Realization and Possession
(xii.a) The king's first dharma is to worship the gods and the Brahmanas, **who are illuminated men.**

The king's second dharma is to be truthful and cover up his weaknesses. The king must send out spies and sow dissension among his enemies.

All men were pure and at peace until lust and covetousness crept in and the world was thrown into darkness. The Vedas lost its influence, so Brahma constructed the Shatras, in a moment, which contained hundred thousand edict on how man should live and perform their religious duties, etc., to cover every aspects of life. It was studied and abridged by the gods, and Shiva being the first. Now they need a ruler to administer the Shastra to the people, and they approached Vishnu. **Vishnu promised to enter into the king's body in order to accomplish his purpose.** This way. the king is endowed with blessing and superior or divine intelligence. *(Mahabharata V2 books 12 & 13 Shanti & Anusasana, 4 Bheeshma's Wisdom)*

Comments: Here is another proof of the doctrine of "spiritual possession" that is referred to as self-realization or illumination in that a person realized the universal self, Atman, or Krishna, etc., the foreign spirit enters the body of the devotee. Here again, it confirmed the fact that Vishnu and Krishna had to enter into the human body, which is in fact a possession by a spiritual or foreign entity.

(xii.b) Krishna claimed that he can come and take a body and go and enjoy the senses and suffer from them as well. *(Mahabharata V2, Book 6 Bheeshma Parva, 8 The song of god)*

Comments: Same as in (xiii) above.

(xiii) Self-Realization and Dispossession

(xiii.a) When a person dies, the light of consciousness exits through the nine gates: two eyes, two nostrils, two ears, mouth, anus, and penis, but the soul is still conscious. Sometime later, two more are added to the nine gates, and they are the navel and the hole (gap joint or sagittal suture) on top of the head or skull, which is called the aperture of Brahma or Brahmarandhra. (That is how Brahma enters the *body*.) *(Bhagavad Gita, chapter 8, The Eternal Godhead, 160)*

Comments: If what the Bhagavad Gita said is true, then all one has to do is to plug up all those holes and Universal Soul or Spirit,

Brahma, Krishna, or the Atman lies trapped inside. So if you just plugged up all the holes before a devotee dies, the Atman is trapped inside and will have to wait until the body rots to escape or when the body is cremated! Does that sound reasonable to you? If the entity is a spirit or a demon, why would it need an opening to enter or exit? When the self-will is destroyed, a foreign entity or spirit can enter or leave as it pleases!

(xiii.b) Those who had abandoned all attachments to the results of their deed attained unified consciousness and supreme peace and is the master of the "nine gates" of the body. (*Bhagavad Gita, chapter 5, Renounce and Rejoice*)
Comments: Same as in (xv.a) above.

(xiii.c) Only the wise see the divine self that dwells or leaves the body and enjoying the sense objects, but the deluded does not. Only those who strive wholeheartedly as a yogi will see the supreme self within. (*Bhagavad Gita, chapter 15, The Supreme Self*)
Comments: In this passage, it talks about a foreign spirit or entity entering or leaving the body.

(xiii.d) When a person dies, the self leaves the body, and the body dies. (*Chandogya Upanishad chapter 6. The story of Shvetaketu 11.3*)
Comments: Here it is talking about the divine self or a foreign entity leaving a body when the body dies. Here the foreign entity of the so-called self is no longer in unity with the individual, there goes all hope of achieving immortality, and all the earlier promises comes to nothing! You had been lied to!

D. Self-Realization and Freedom from Attachments

(i) Attainment of the perfect yoga
Those who live by the fruits if their achievements are miserable. When the consciousness is unified. it is free from all attachments. When your mind overcomes the dualities of life, you attain a state of indifference to all things, and you are unmoved by confusion,

then you have attained the perfect yoga. *(Bhagavad Gita, chapter 2, Self-Realization)*

Comments: What the Ghagavad Gita or Krishna does not tell you is that it may take several lifetimes or Samsara cycles and that you may not be where you are at in the next lifetime and that you may have devolved. Furthermore, there is no evidence to substantiate or guarantee that you will be back to earth in the next lifetime or if there is a next lifetime at all. And if not, then you had really screwed up this one, and there is no recourse!

(ii) Freedom from all attachments

When you are free from all attachments, then you live in the full wisdom of the self. Then you had renounced all selfish desires and break free from the I, Me, and Mine. which is united with the Lord, and that is the supreme state, and it passes from death into immortality. *(Bhagavad Gita, chapter 2, Self-Realization)*

Comments: The fact that one needs to eat solid food and drink water tells you that the person is still attached to the needs of the flesh. Further to that, the person wears any clothes tells you that he is affected by heat and cold and is therefore not free from the effects of the elements, thus attached to his bodily needs. He or she will be totally free when he is dead! This doctrine also implies that the devotee becomes free of devotion, affection, love, wife, parents, and children or babies! He has no need for them and would leave them destitute in order for his desire to be as One or in Unity with god or the Atman. How do you feel about it? If you broke free of I, then you cannot say I love you as there is no I! Krishna is already fully realized, so when he said he loves you, it is an impossibility because he had renounce the I.

(iii) Krishna the Divine Self

Krishna defined himself as the divine self found in everyone and cannot be reborn. To discover the divine self in you is to be delivered form all selfish attachments, fear, and anger and in that way is purified in the fire of Krishna's being and is in unity with Krishna. *(Bhagavad Gita, chapter 4, Wisdom in Action)*

Comments: Brahma claimed the same thing that he is the divine self and is in everyone, so who are you going to believe? Two deities are claiming the same. so one or both are lying. Krishna was killed by a deer hunter as in the Mahabharata and can be found in chapter 7E section P (ii), and that Krishna did not resurrect nor was there any record that he was rebirthed. If Krishna is the divine self and found in everyone, why is there a need to enter into someone or another body as in section above?

(iv) Complete control by Krishna

When the mind, sense, and body are controlled by the self (Krishna), he is indeed free from all attachments, external supports, anxiety, expectations, all sense of possessions, results, and all desires. *(Bhagavad Gita, chapter 4, Wisdom in Action)*

Comments: This doctrine confessed the truth that it is the self, Krishna, Atman, or a spiritual entity that is actually taking over the control of the person and confirming that it is spiritual possession! When a person is possessed, he or she no longer has control over his or her bodily functions. You can see evidences in some extreme cases when possessed folks are obsessed with cutting themselves or casting themselves into the fire, etc. However, many possessions are evidenced by personality disorder, and sometimes addictions, etc. Modern-day psychiatry called it multiple personality disorder, which is true as there are other personalities in the person possessed.

(v) Dualities of Life

(v.a) Atman and the Dualities of Life

Krishna reminded Arjuna that his true self, the Atman, is eternal and is never born or die, but the soul travels from one birth to another. It is in the Samsara cycle, and it is not subject to time and death. In order to see the truth, one must see past the dualities of life: pleasure and pain, success and failure, or even hot or cold. The intent of the Gita is to teach one the path of detachment from the dualities of life and identify with the Atman, the immortal self. *(Bhagavad Gita, chapter 2, Self-Realization)*

Comments: It seems that the attainment of self-realization is definitely not for those who lack the intellectual capability and mental toughness to see and understand the duality of life; therefore, the folks who are not that smart can never attain immortality. It also means that if you lack those qualities, immortality is not for you. It is unfair to those who are not born with those qualities!

(v.b) The duality of attachment and aversion deceives and confuses the mind right from birth, and the only way to escape this delusion is by devotion to Krishna. *(Bhagavad Gita, chapter 7, Wisdom & Realization)*

Comments: As shown in the preceding comments, Krishna is not able to sever all attachments nor assist the suppression of them. And for those who failed in freeing themselves from their attachments, Krishna has no love for them, as can be found in section H (xvii) below.

(v.c) The one who is dear to Krishna are those that had conquered the dualities of life and are unmoved by anything that life dishes out. They are pure, detached, efficient, impartial, never anxious and selfless, and are Krishna's devotees. *(Bhagavad Gita, chapter 12, The way of Love)*

Comments: Same as in (xv) above.

(v.d) Knowledge is better than mechanical practice, but meditation is better than knowledge. However, better still is the surrender of attachment to results because one attains immediate peace. **The ones that I, Krishna, loves are those you live beyond the dualities of life** like pleasure and pain, and beyond the I and mine, in self-control, focused on faith and had given me all their heart and their mind to me. *(Bhagavad Gita, chapter 12, The way Love)*

Comments: Just remember, Krishna does not love the 99.999 percent of all Hindus but only those who are free of attachments! To surrender the heart and mind means total possession! That means you no longer have a mind of your own nor have your own longings or desire of your own. You ceased to be yourself with no individuality.

(v.e) A person who is free from the dualities of life and perform all their selfless service, their karma is dissolved. Brahman is attached by those who see Brahman in every action. *(Bhagavad Gita, chapter 4, Wisdom in Action)*

Comments: There needs to be a clarification here, in that *selfless* does not mean unselfish but that once the "self or the self-will' had been destroyed and is possessed, then anything that comes from it is without the true self; otherwise, it is impossible not to be selfish or still possess the dualities of life.

(vi) Spiritual Wisdom in the Divine Self or Krishna

The knowledge of spiritual wisdom will dissolve karma and purifies and attains perfect peace.

Those who had found the divine self (Krishna) in themselves can never be happy in this world. They had renounced all selfish attachments and have no doubts in them and using the sword of spiritual wisdom will take the path of yoga. *(Bhagavad Gita, chapter 4, Wisdom in Action)*

Comments: Here Krishna is defining what happiness is! All selfish attachments include parents, wife, sons and daughters, babies, house, cars, bicycles, etc. makes the devotee unhappy or is without happiness! Is that spiritual wisdom to leave your loved ones destitute and go begging for food and clothes to wear?

(vii) Two Paths to Self-Realization

(vii.a) There are two paths toward self-realization. The self is Krishna (Avatara of Vishnu), and to self-realize is to realize or discover the Krishna (or Vishnu) in you. The two paths are (a) renunciation or sannyasa and (b) selfless service. To renounce is to leave family, home, work, friends and live an austere life of a monk. The life of selfless service is a life of action with no attachment to the results or forsaking the dualities of life. *(Bhagavad Gita, chapter 5, Renounce and Rejoice)*

Comments: Any path to self-realization is to fully surrender and become vulnerable to the entry of a foreign spirit or entity into the person. And that is spiritual possession.

(vii.b) To be free from selfish attachments is to be free from home and family and seek only the true divine self; otherwise, it is ignorance. *(Bhagavad Gita, chapter 13, The Field & the Knower)*

Comments: Please read comments in (vii.a)

(vii.c) Those who are liberated and achieved self-realization lives with Krishna and do not return to a separate existence. The divine self enters at conception and leaves the body when death arrives. The divine self uses the all the sense and enjoys the sense objects. *(Bhagavad Gita, chapter 15, The Supreme Self)*

Comments: How is it possible to commit your life to self-realization and leave your family destitute for want of food, shelter, and clothing for a life of enlightenment? To forsake your responsibilities for the children you are partly responsible is recklessness and a total disregard for the welfare of your offspring! They should be thrown into prison where they can meditate and contemplate all they want.

(viii) Surrendering to the Divine Self or Krishna

(viii.a) Those who surrendered to the divine spirit or Brahman is free of all selfish attachments and cannot be touched by sin. *(Bhagavad Gita, chapter 5, Renounce and Rejoice)*

(viii.b)Those who had abandoned all attachments to the results of their deed attained unified consciousness and supreme peace and is the master of the "nine gates" of the body. *(Bhagavad Gita, chapter 5, Renounce and Rejoice)*

(viii.c) The true divine self in a person is not affected by whether the deed done is good or bad because it has no attachment to results. The illuminated person sees the divine self in all, regardless. *(Bhagavad Gita, chapter 5, Renounce and Rejoice)*

Comments: What this means is that in total detachment or renunciation, you are not affected by all the societal misery, disasters, murders, and mayhem around you because you are in total peace. You do not need to have sympathy or empathy or provide aid or helping hand to those who needed them because you cease to have feeling for them. Finally, you have arrived and is divine and illuminated! Being totally devoid of empathy is not human as from empathy comes mercy, sacrifice, acts of love, charity, etc.! And being at one with the self, Krishna, or Atman, one is devoid of all that is precious in life! Can a coconut or mango tree produce anything but coconuts and mangoes? How is the sin nature severed from the person is never mentioned in the Bhagavad Gita, and saying it is so does not make it true.

(ix) Knowledge of the Divine Self or Krishna

Krishna does not take part in the good or evil deeds of a person. The knowledge of the self (Krishna) within destroys ignorance and reveals the supreme Brahman within. And those who threw out sin is absorbed into the Lord Krishna. *(Bhagavad Gita, chapter 5, Renounce and Rejoice)*

Comments: This statement is false as Krishna actually partook in the war as described in the Mahabharata by taking side with Arjuna. And Krishna admitted that he perjured himself in the Ramayana, and how is that not sin or evil? Why does Krishna marry 16,108 women, as in the Padma and Vishnu Puranas, having no feelings, love, desire for them at all?

(x) United mind with the Divine Self or Brahman

(x.a) Those whose mind is united with the Brahman or the divine self in himself is free from delusion and, with a unified consciousness through meditation, live in abiding joy. *(Bhagavad Gita, chapter 5, Renounce and Rejoice)*

Comments: It is a contradictory statement in that Shiva, Vishnu, Brahma, Krishna, and Indra are all full of deceptions and delusions, so how then is it possible to be free of delusion when you become united with any of them. Further to that, when one is free of all attachments, especially in this case your feelings, how are you able to live in joy as joy requires feelings and emotions and the reflections of elated emotions of being happy.

(x.b) All dualities of life end up in misery. When united with the Brahman, in themselves they attained Nirvana and find joy and rest within themselves. Free from the dualities of life through the path of yoga, the self is established forever in a supreme state. Meditation with closed eyes and steadying breath, focusing on the center of spiritual consciousness, the devotee will master their senses, mind, intellect with self-realization as their only goal that attain eternal peace. (*Bhagavad Gita, chapter 5, Renounce and Rejoice*)

Comments: I can assure you that most of the world are able to handle the dualities of life and are not miserable. We do enjoy companies, have celebrations, and take vacations so it is a big jump to say that all dualities of life end up in misery. If they had attained Nirvana, why are they still stuck on earth and require sustenance of food and water and therefore not free of attachments! What a deceiving and contrary doctrine in that Hindus have more celebrations and festivals than any religious groups on earth, and because of them, being involved in the dualities of life will all end up being the most miserable!

(x.c) A man who realized the Brahman is always united with the Brahman never wanders as his soul is yoked with the Brahman. Nothing can affect the yogin, no material things, no joy, no pain, no sorrow, no desire or lust, nor anger. The body, mind, and life is pure, and he achieved eternal bliss as natural as breathing. (*Mahabharata vol. 2 book 6: Bheeshma Parva, 5 The song of god*)

Comments: As described, the man who realized the Brahman is of no use or benefit to society, as he does not feel the pain, the sorrow, the hurt, for the starving, etc. of those around him and therefore unable to help. He cannot help unless he recognizes the needs around him, but he cannot because he is always in eternal bliss. A crying and starving baby he cannot help because he is always in a state of bliss and has no feeling or attachment. To be affected by the misery around you is to have a tender heart, which a realized Brahman does not have! You will not be equally yoked with Brahman because he is superior to you, and therefore you will always serve him and be under bondage. If a starving hungry baby had no effect on a Brahman or a Hindu deity, then they are both monsters or demons and not god!

(x.d) Krishna identified the senses, and they are pleasure, pain, desire, revulsion, the entire organism, intelligence, will, humility, honest, patience, nonviolence, self-effacement, and perception and they can be classified under that of the body and of the mind. Krishna provides the guideline to lead a person to being a Brahman, and they are as follows: detachment from all things, no dependence on a wife, children or a home, and absolute nonfeeling to pleasure or pain; total devotion to me, a life in solitary parts, far from the crowd; constancy in the yoga and insight. **The Brahma is transcendent and has no beginning or end, eternal that is. He is and is not. He sees, hears, and senses all things. But he does not feel a thing at all, no joy nor sorrow. He is totally unattached and is free of his nature but enjoys nature.** Regardless of how a man lives, if he had experienced the Brahman directly, then, beyond nature, he will never be reborn. (*Mahabharata vol. 2 book 6: Bheeshma Parva 7 The Bhagavad Gita*)

Comments: Krishna was born the eighth child born to Vasudeva and Devaki but fostered out to Yashoda and Nand and was the eighth Avatar of Vishnu and therefore had a beginning, and that Krishna was killed by a deer hunter or Ventala, named Jara, as in Mahabharata story, and there he had a beginning and an end. No one ever saw Krishna rose from the dead. According to the same criteria in the doctrine preached, Krishna is not illuminated or had attained the Atman or the Universal Soul or Spirit, and that means Krishna is not eternal.

You already know that the claim is incorrect as Brahma was full of lust and desire of Shiva's bride and ejaculated his semen. If a preacher or teacher and his teachings are not in unity or harmony, then it hides a lie. And liars cannot be trusted! So how can you believe the doctrines found in the Bhagavad Gita?

(xi) Freedom from Old Age and Death

Those who seek to be free from old age and death and take refuge in Krishna will be united with the Brahman, and the divine self will be conscious of Krishna at the time of death. (*Bhagavad Gita, chapter 7, Wisdom & Realization*)

Comments: Here lies the contradiction to what Krishna, the eighth avatar or Vishnu, is teaching, in that Rama, the seventh avatar of Vishnu committed suicide by walking into the fire! And Krishna himself is killed by a deer hunter in the Mahabharata. Both of them never discovered old age. Committing suicide is a final and ultimate action which reflected the surrender to the hopelessness of a situation, with the inability to control its outcome. And here Rama, an avatar of Vishnu a god, had no control of a situation and is totally helpless and hopeless. So why would you want to worship Rama or Vishnu or even Krishna, as he also is an avatar of Vishnu?

(xii) Benefits of total devotion to Krishna

(xii.a) If one can be total devoted to Krishna alone, the purity of the will alone will free the person from his selfish motives and release him from his karma, and his spirit will be free to have union with Krishna. *(Bhagavad Gita, chapter 9, The Royal Path)*

Comments: Some folks have lots and lots of money and lived a privileged life. Why would they want to go to heaven as they already have heaven on earth? Just the begging poor who does not want to come back to this miserable life, but there is no guarantee where they will go after death. In Hinduism, there is no guarantee or assurance as to where a person will go after death. Only those who are able to meditate day and night to detach themselves of their desires and wants are promised with life with their god, but again there is no guarantee nor proof. In the meantime, they neglected the care of their wives and children and deign them to poverty and constant hunger.

(xii.b) When a person comes to know his universal self or atman and his soul, he is set free from all desires, and torments of his heart disappear. When a person is totally absorbed in his universal self or atman, he is enlightened, therefore is wise. Desire, lust, fear, rage, or evil have no effect or hold on him, and he becomes a Brahmanrishi, the enlightened one. When he dies, he achieves the eternal enlightenment and is one with god. Krishna's advice to Arjuna is let war be your worship. *(Mahabharata V2 book 6: Bheeshma Parva, 4 Bhagavad Gita)*

Comments: Here is another lie, as it is not "his" Universal Self or Atman, but that it is in reality a foreign spiritual entity that had to enter a person to possess him or her. It had already been proven that all these characters, Krishna, Brahma, Shiva, Indra, Vishnu, are deceivers and all for the intent to possess a body and control the devotee. Krishna perjured himself, Indra raped, Shiva and Brahma both cannot control their sexual emotions and ejaculated at the person to whom they are attracted to. Are these the examples the devotees are supposed to follow?

E. Self-realization and Renunciation

(i) Introduction: Renunciation and free of attachments are the two sides of the same coin in that it is part and parcel of how a person can attain self-realization. This is the first or initial step, but it was found inadequate, and it encountered tremendous roadblocks in that it was unable to destroy the self-will. They tried and tried but continually failed over the years, and that is until they found out or discovered that with meditation, it was able to break down the protective wall of the self-will. And from just plain meditation, it progressed into Yogic meditation, where it is finally able to break down or destroy the protective wall of the self-will, as stated in *The Shvetashvatara Upanishad, as mentioned below in section C (iii)*.

All these renunciation and being free of attachments are men's attempts at achieving self-righteousness in order to be able to attain immortality and be at one with God or be as God. This has always been man's quest since day one: to be as God. You can call it by any other name like being in union with, etc., but the lie or the deception is the same. The temptation of being "as God" comes with many and all kinds of attractive end goals that men find hard to resist; the fruits of the tree are almost impossible to resist to men, to achieve perfection and be as one or union with God and, therefore, immortality. The God of the Bible says that your righteousness is as filthy rags. In order for Hinduism to achieve immortality and union with God is to make God smaller, with less expectations and be like men.

There is a noble attempt at being perfect and attaining righteousness through "works" to be able to renounce all desires and wants as well as being free of all attachments, including parents and children, but it is a foolish and futile attempt. The minute you think you had achieved this goal, pride creeps in. Even if you achieve that status for an hour while in the midst of your meditation, the minute you step out into the world, you will sin. Unless you get rid of the root for sin, sin is always there, like your DNA, that it is impossible to get rid of it. So what are listed below are all the promises to be able to achieve unity with and, thus be as, God. It is just vanity of vanities.

(ii) Two kinds of Renunciation

There are two kinds of renunciation, the sannyasa (the rejection of selfish acts) and tsaya (self-sacrifice, giving, and self-discipline). The act of tyasa should not be renounced because they purify the person, and it should be performed without selfish desires or rewards. (*Bhagavad Gita, chapter 18, Freedom & Renunciation*)

Comments: The minute you feel satisfied with sannyasa or tsaya, you fail because being satisfied is self-gratification, and if you are never successful in whatever you embark upon, then you fail. It becomes a catch 22 a quandary for the believers or devotees. The reason for the quandary or confusion, is because the minute you 'feel or sense' that you had achieved success then you had *not* cut yourself off from having feelings or emotions, which is contrary to the teaching of renunciation. It is futile attempt at self-righteousness through so-called righteous works.

(iii) Freedom to Kill

(iii.a) A person who has a pure heart and free from ego, though he kills, is not responsible for his action. (*Bhagavad Gita, chapter 18, Freedom and Renunciation*)

Comments: Even Shiva lusted (*Shiva Purana 5.3 Shatruda Samhita 5:3:19 Incarnation of Hanuman*), Brahma lusted (*Vamana Purana 6:17 Birth of Uma and her marriage to Shiva 6.17.3 Uma Marries Lord Shiva*), and both of them ejaculated at the object of their lust. Indra raped King Maharishi Gautama's wife Ahalya (*Ramayana Book 1 Bala Kanda 14. Rishi Gautama's asrama*), and Krishna knowingly lied as in the *Mahabharata V2, Book 7 Droan Parva, 12 Arjuna's Dream p 323*. If they, being gods, are unable to have a pure heart and free from ego, what chance do you think you have? If they cannot break the bonds of their sin DNA, then I feel sad to tell you that your chance of achieving full self-realization is exactly one big fat zero! All three gods, Brahma, Shiva, and Vishnu, compete to see who is number one, so how is any of these gods be free from ego and is pure of heart? This doctrine is also justifying killing without feeling guilty. Adolf Hitler and Joseph Stalin can claim that they have a pure heart and free from ego, which justified their killing of millions in Europe. It is evident and apparent that they are free from feelings and attachments!

(iii.b) The teachings of the Upanishads are that there are five components to any work or deed, and they are the ego, sense, body, action, and providence, and everything is caused by these five components. He who has the idea that he is the one who acts is delusional. But the person who is unattached at all, free of egotism, and acted naturally and perfectly, no karma is able to impose or dictate his life, and **even though he kills one thousand, he is not a killer.** *(Mahabharata vol. 2, book 6 Bheeshma Parva, 9 The Bhagavad Gita)*

Comments: Here the doctrine is teaching that a person, who is free of all attachments, is not guilty even if he kills one thousand. This is really a dangerous doctrine. Who then is the judge to say that the person who killed one thousand is not free of attachments? Who is to say that Adolf Hitler, Joseph Stalin, Gen. Pol Pot were not free of attachments? Actually, they were all free of conscience in all that they had done! Were they then free of all attachments and were fully realized? They claimed that they had fulfilled their dharma!

(iv) Mastering Renunciation

For those who had mastered renunciation from all things, desires, lusts, anger, self-will, and selfishness will enter into a unitive state with Krishna and **will always be joyful,** beyond the reach of desire and sorrow and attained supreme devotion to Krishna. And by loving Krishna, they will truly know him and will perform all acts in his service and through his grace wins eternal life.

Comments: According to the Chandogya Upanishad (Prajapati Instructions to Indra and Virochana), it took Indra 105 years to be master of the skill, and he still failed. And if it took Indra 105 years and failed. What chance do you think you have? How can you possibly master the art of renunciation and still love Krishna as you are by now totally void of any feeling? To love anything or anyone requires a deep feeling or emotion and commitment of the heart. It is impossible to destroy the emotion and then be joyful. It sounds like double talk, and you cannot love Krishna because if you succeeded in destroying your true self with complete renunciation, then the self is destroyed and therefore the self ceases to exist and cannot love! The intent of this doctrine is for you to destroy your self-will so that the foreign entity or spirit can enter and possess your body!

(v) The Instructions of Renunciation Is Directly from Lord Krishna

The Gita is the supreme secret and wisdom for the supreme union directly from the Lord of yoga, Krishna himself. *(Bhagavad Gita, chapter 18, Freedom & Renunciation)*

Comments: If Krishna is already in everything, then he is in you already and therefore in union, so why is there a need to be in union again? According to the Mahabharata story, he is in everything animate and inanimate, so why is there a need for union? Why is there a need for Krishna or the foreign entity or spirit to enter or possess the body as per the *The Shvetashvatara Upanishad quoted below?*

Self-Realization, Yoga, and Mantram
(viii) **He (Brahma) is the source of all the powers of life.** *He is the Lord of all,* **the great seer**
Who dwells forever in the cosmic womb.
May **he purify our consciousness.**
O Lord (Brahma) in whom alone we can find peace,
May we see your divine Self and **be freed**
From all impure thoughts and all fear.
O Lord, from whom we receive the mantram
As a weapon to destroy our self-will,

Reveal yourself, protector of all. *(The Shvetashvatara Upanishad)*

Comments: Herein lies the truth about the purpose of intense meditation, yogic or otherwise, and the continuous chants or mantram in that it dulls the mind and weakens the hearts and destroy the self-will so that the "foreign entity," like Krishna, Brahma, Atman, etc. can enter into the devotee. I had termed it as possession by a foreign spirit. Therein lies the deception. Krishna, Brahma, Shiva, and Vishna had been shown in the Hindu sacred texts that they are DECEIVERS, and here is the deception, that under the pretense of an individual achieving IMMORTALITY by being in union with Krishna or Brahma or the lot, the person is actually getting possessed by a foreign spirit.

(vi) Doomed for Failure Without Krishna

Regardless of how you try to resist your karma, you will fail unless you worship and meditate on me, regard me as your sole protector as I will set you free form your karma and your delusions. To fight this battle all on your own, you will fail as your own karma will drive you to it by your delusion, and you are only free when Krishna is your refuge and your lord. *(Bhagavad Gita, chapter 18, Freedom & Renunciation)*

Comments: In this doctrine, a person born a Shudra of the lowest caste cannot get out of it by had work or by using his intelligence. It seems like a curse than a doctrine. It seems that the present-day Indian government is acting contrary to the great Hindu tradition of the caste system. It is disobeying Krishna and Brahma as they both claimed to create the Indian caste system. What are the consequences of disobeying the great gods Brahma and Krishna? What comes out of a god's mouth must be truth and commandment, and how can disobeying their mandate be without penalties?

(vii) The Three Gunas

(vi.a) All things, actions, or thought can be classified into Sattvic, Rajasic, or Tamasic, be it understanding, happiness, etc. For more on **Sattvic, Rajasic, and Tamastic,** please read (vii) and (xi). *(Bhagavad Gita, chapter 18, Freedom & Renunciation)* (vi.b) Krishna defines renunciation as the election to abandon one's karma, and relinquishment is to abandon the results of one's action. **Therefore, the wise, in order to purify themselves, must perform the sacrifice**, penance, and charity with no attachments to the results. Renunciation through ignorance is **tamasic**, and through fear is **rajasic**, and finally if through abandonment of the outcome is sattvasic. The sattvic is able to distinguish right from wrong or what is safe from what is dangerous. The rajasic cannot tell right from wrong and what to do or not do, but the tamasic thinks evil is good and lives in delusion. *(Mahabharata Vol. 2, book 6 Bheeshma Parva, 9 The Bhagavad Gita)*

Comments: Krishna had already said the Vedic practices are inferior to self-realization and yet here, Krishna is asking the devotee to practice a sacrifice, which is a Vedic practice. It seems that purification is necessary for sins or evil acts and thoughts, etc. How is it possible to cleanse oneself from sins and evil acts or thoughts through sacrifice, penance, or charity without attachments as the act or acts are already committed? Who is offended by the sins, evil acts or thoughts? Who had the offender committed the offense against? If it is god, then which god? What if the gods, like Krishna, Shiva, Vishna, Brahma, and Indra, who committed the offense, who are they offending and who should they do their penance or sacrifice to?

(vi.c) Sages, who had become perfect like him, Krishna, is freed from the bonds of the body. They are not born by creation and therefore cannot be destroyed in the dissolution. Everyone that is born in this world had his seed from Krishna, and Prakriti is the mother.

Krishna defines the three gunas: Sattva (goodness, constructive, and harmonious), Tamas (darkness, chaotic, and destructive), and Rajas (passionate, active, and confused). At different times, one will dominate the other. The soul attains a higher world when a person is dominated by sattva. The soul is deluded and devolved into a lower world if tamas dominates when a person dies. Finally, a person will be reborn again into actions and passion if the rajas dominate when a person dies.

Every word of Krishna is scripture! A person who is free from desire, lusts, pleasure, pain, and delusion and conquered the evil of attachments of material and immaterial things has attained Krishna and cannot be reborn again. *(Mahabharata Vol. 2 book 6: Bheeshma Parva 7 The Bhagavad Gita)*

Comments: How can you possibly believe in Krishna when he already tells you that he is a DECEIVER and the "lord of the Maya" as in the *Bhagavad Gita*, chapter 7, Wisdom and Realization, you would realize the Krishna is far from perfect and therefore the above is a lie?

F. Self-Realization and Selfless Service

(i) Introduction: There needs to be a clarification here in that "self-less" does not mean unselfishness but that once the self-will had been destroyed and anything that comes from it is without self, otherwise it is impossible not to be selfish or still possess the dualities of life. Further to that, when the self-will is destroyed, the person is filled with the Atman, Universal Soul, Spirit, or foreign entity and sometimes called the SELF, so to attain self-realization is to possess the Atman or termed the "self." It is a very cunning or deceptive way of playing with words that only the Deceiver can contrive.

(ii) Freedom from the three gunas

(ii.a) A spiritual life progresses from tamas to rajas to sattvas, and the final is to be free of the three gunas and achieve the Atman or universal self. *(Bhagavad Gita, chapter 3, Selfless Service)*

Comments: It is very difficult for anyone to possess, behave, or act solely with just one gunas, but that a person is a mixture or combination of all three gunas. Therefore, to say that a person's spiritual life progresses from the tamas to the rajas and finally to the sattvas is a false notion or misconception. Even as one is "good" or does "good," evil is found in him, even though it is nascent.

(ii.b) The field is made up of the five sense areas of perception; five sense organs, and five organs of action. The three divisions of the mind are the memory (manas), intelligence and understanding (bud-dhi), and the ego with its self-will (ahamkara). In the field, a person experiences the dualities of life, but detached he will be truly free of it all and suffering, old age, disease, and continual deaths and rebirths. *(Bhagavad Gita, chapter 13, The Field & the Knower)*

Comments: Same as in (xiii.c) above.

(ii.c) **There is no spiritual growth without self-discipline.** Tapas or tap means heat or suffering. When spiritual practices are mastered, there is a feeling of heat in the body, also termed as tapas, which is a sign of increased spiritual potency and power gained through austerity. The sattvic tapas leads the person to his spiritual goal. The rajasic tapas is performed for selfish gains and admiration from others, and the tamasic tapas deludes and a person will suffer pain with foolish practices for gain of power and even to injure other. *(Bhagavad Gita, chapter 17, The Power of Faith)*

Comments: Here spiritual growth means that you get more and more successful toward full renunciation and free of attachments and having no feelings at all. Yes, of course, it takes relentless discipline to spend a tremendous amount of time to continually be in meditation to be successful, but to what end? To be like a piece or log or rock? The gaining of spiritual potency or power is just another bait as what does it really mean? Will the spiritual potency or power allow you to function as a deity or god, and in this case, as that of a spiritual entity or demon? Can you cure the sick, heal the blind, or walk on water? The disciples and followers of Jesus, as in the Christian Bible, are able to raise the dead, cast out demons, heal the lame and sick, and perform many other miracles without fierce meditation, tapasya, or self-realization but are given power by the Holy Spirit of God through Christ Jesus as promised in the Word of God, which is the Christian Bible.

(ii.d) Vishnu said: **Only very few in this world are able to control their sensual desires and attain self-realization.** Relentless effort must be made to acquire divine knowledge of self-realization as all other knowledge is superficial and insignificant. When desire is extinguished he will experience the divine state of self-realization. A person can be influenced by his sensual perception into believing that what he senses is real and failed to know and understand the real cause for the existence of this world, and that is not true for a person who is fully realized. Instead of searching for what is outside, he should seek for what is within himself. With a pure heart and relentless pursuit, he will attain self-realization. Vishnu went on to say that he is pure and beyond the limits of human intelligence and is beyond the confinement of the three gunas, sattva, raja, and tamas, and only the enlightened soul can experience him and drive away the darkness. *(Garuda Purana 14.13 Salvation through yoga 14.13.1 Self-Realization)*

Comments: Yes indeed, only the very, very few can attain self-realization, maybe less than .01 percent of all Hindus or even less are capable to achieving that goal. But then, why does Vishnu, Shiva, Brahma, and Krishna make it so difficult for the 99.99 percent of the population, such that they are stuck in the Samsara cycle and return to lives of misery and suffering. The doctrine required moral perfection for the imperfect human, requiring him or her to exist as a piece of wood or rock. This doctrine of self-realization promotes the earning of self-righteousness while stuck in sin and desires without the ability to sever them both. For the Hindu, there is no guarantee of eternal life as he or she does not know if his or her self-righteous works are adequate, which is very different for the Christian and biblical doctrine, where there is an assurance of their sins being forgiven and eternal life guaranteed.

(iii) Selfless Service

(iii.a) Selfless service imprisons the world. Fulfilment of your desires is in selfless service as promised by the Creator. Honour and cherish the devas: (a) they will return in kind, (b) you will attain supreme good, and (c) they will fulfil all your human desires, who are pleased with your selfless service. *(Bhagavad Gita, chapter 3, Selfless Service)*

Comments: The statement is contradictory because there cannot be a fulfilment of one's desire because to attain the Atman or

Universal Self, one must be devoid of desire, so how then is it possible to fulfil what is not there?

(iii.b) When a person eats in the spirit of selfless service, he is freed from all sins, and those who eat for self-satisfaction eats sins. All selfless act comes from the eternal Brahma as he is present in every act of self service. *(Bhagavad Gita, chapter 3, Selfless Service)*

Comments: To suppress sin does not mean it is not there. It just meant it is suppressed. What is there to sever a person from the root of sin embedded in his DNA? So how then is a person free from all sins if the root of sin is not severed?

(iii.c) All work attached with any of the three gunas is from the ego and is therefore attached to it, but selfless service is free of the gunas. *(Bhagavad Gita, chapter 3, Selfless Service)*

Comments: If there is no desire, need, wants, or feelings, then there is no service. It is like a piece of rock or log; it has no need, no wants, no desires, no feelings, and as a result it just sits there and do nothing whether there be rain or shine. Therefore, the piece of rock or log had truly ascended and achieved full illumination or self-realization.

(iii.d) It is selfish desires in the senses, mind, and intellect that mislead and delude a person; therefore, it is necessary to control all the senses, mind, and intellect. That which is higher than the senses, mind, and intellect is the Atman or the eternal self. *(Bhagavad Gita, chapter 3, Selfless Service)*

Comments: The foreign entity like the Atman or Universal Self may indeed have higher senses, mind, or intellect than you. But that does not mean it will serve the ultimate good, and it is a great possibility that it is evil in nature. Yes, evil, you must have had read that the so-called Hindu deities fight with each other for dominance due to the lack of sexual self-control, lies, and deception, which indeed is evil! So why would you allow them to control your mind, senses, and intellect?

(iv) The Path of a Brahman

Only selfless service in the path of a Brahman will attain liberation and will never again be deluded and will see the self (Krishna) in everything. *(Bhagavad Gita, chapter 4, Wisdom in Action)*

Comments: It is impossible not to be deluded because the self or Krishna himself is the lord of the Maya or delusions or lies, and if you are in union with him, then you too are a deceiver and a liar!

G. Self-Realization and Yoga

(i) Introduction

The yogic posture is in reality a serpentine pose. The crossover of the legs represents the serpent's coil. The upright position on the spine is as the upright position of the cobra when upright. And in this yogic position, the energy in the position is called the Kundalini energy or serpent energy. This is all in agreement with the following Hindu gods: (a) Vishnu rests on Ananta or Sheshnaga, the serpent, (b) Shiva has Vasuki coiled around his body or neck, and (c) Krishna claimed to be both Ananta and Vasuki. In reality, Vishnu, Shiva, and Krishna are but personifications of the serpent, and that is consistent with the yogic posture, whereby the Kundalini energy is quickened.

(ii) Krishna, the first teacher of Yoga

Krishna proclaimed that he, in his past life, taught yoga to Vivasat (sun), who in turn taught it to Manu, the offspring of Brahma and Shatrupa (Brahma's creation) or Saraswati. Brahma (god) created Ananti who married Manu, and both became parents to humans. Yoga was passed on until it was lost. *(Bhagavad Gita, chapter 5, Renounce and Rejoice)*

Comments: Krishna had claimed many things about himself, including the fact that he is the lord of the maya or illusion or deception and is therefore a master liar. Would you believe in a liar? Would you believe in or trust your wife, parents, or children if you know they are a liar? If not, why would you trust in a god who lies or deceives?

(iii) The three types of yoga are (a) Gyan yoga, (b) Kriya yoga, and (c) Bhakti yoga. Gyan yoga is when the mind unites with the soul. Kriya is when the soul is attached to external objects, and Bhakti is when the whole being is united with the goddess Bhagawati. **All three types of yoga will give salvation to the devotee.** (*5.5 Uma Samhita 5.6.1 Classifications of Yoga*)

Comments: All three types of yoga serve the same ultimate purpose and that is to achieve union with the Universal Self or Spirit, the Atman, receives Illumination or Enlightenment, and therefore be as one with God and attain immortality. And yet, in Hinduism's own sacred text, it tells the truth that the practice ultimately destroys the self-will, as in section C (iii) and that the foreign spirit can enter the person through the crown of the head or sagittal aperture, as in section C (iii, x, and xi).

(iv) Only the Very Few Can Attain Self-Realization

Vishnu said: Only very few in this world are able to control their sensual desires and attain self-realization. Relentless effort must be made to acquire divine knowledge of self-realization as all other knowledge is superficial and insignificant. When desire is extinguished in the will, he experiences the divine state of self-realization. A person can be influenced by his sensual perception into believing that what he senses is real and fail to know and understand the real cause for the existence of this world, and that is not true for a person, who is fully realized. Instead of searching for what is outside, he should seek for what is within himself. With a pure heart and relentless pursuit, he will attain self-realization. Vishnu went on to say that he is pure and beyond the limits of human intelligence and is beyond the confinement of the three gunas, sattva, raja, and tamas, and only the enlightened soul can experience him and drive away the darkness. (*Garuda Purana 14.13 Salvation through yoga 14.13.1 Self-Realization*)

Comments: As mentioned, very few in Hinduism achieved self-realization, illumination, enlightenment, union with the self or Atman, and therefore the hundreds of millions of Hindus are deign for rebirths, some to go higher and others to devolve. So they are not a happy lot, as there is no surety for salvation or guarantee in the afterlife, as they are unable to completely deny or shunt their family, wife, and children and dedicate themselves to the life of yogic meditation. It is a shame that they cannot have total renunciation or free of attachments, as they have to take a break to eat or drink and perform bodily functions and to support and provide for your family!

(v) The principles of Yoga is to break through the bonds of karma, and there is no failure nor waste, and it will protect you from your worst fears. See me alone with a single purpose, and you will achieve the self. *(Bhagavad Gita, chapter 2, Self-Realization)*

Comments: It seems that only those who can spend time in yogic meditation until the self-will and desire are destroyed can attain immortality. For the rest of the common men and women who had to go out to make a living by putting food on the table instead of meditation, immortality is elusive. And the irony is that the common working men and women had to work their butt of, and the meditating priests would come begging for food or alms from working folks, and the result is the begging priest attained immortality, and the working poor is stuck with the Samsara cycle. The begging priests are in actual fact society's parasites, so they can attain their selfish needs of immortality and neglect the care of their parents, wife, and babies or children! This is very different from Christianity in that the promise and assurance of eternal salvation comes through faith in the belief that Jesus, the begotten Son of God the Father, gave His life for a sacrifice on the cross for sin that all may inherit eternal life for those, who believe.

(vi) The Two Paths of Yoga

(v.a) There are two paths for a pure of heart: (a) jnana yoga, a contemplative path to spiritual wisdom and (b) Karma yoga, a path of selfless service. And both require action. *(Bhagavad Gita, chapter 3, Selfless Service)*

Comments: Either paths are not free of sin even as the process of denial is the suppression of sin, desire, wants, needs, feelings, etc. To suppress is not to cut off, and therefore, sin is latent in the devotee though it does not show itself. Therefore, either path is not pure but is tainted. Here it is teaching that a pure heart can be achieved through works for the attainment of self-realization whereas the Christian scriptures says that salvation is by grace, a gift of God, which is free, and not of works, lest any men should boast.

(v.b) Once you know the two paths, light and darkness, to liberation or to rebirths, you can never be deluded again. **This knowledge can only be attained through constant yogic meditation.** There are merits in studying the scriptures, austerity, selfless service, giving alms, **but the practice of meditation surpasses all** and attains union with Krishna. *(Bhagavad Gita, chapter 8, The Eternal Godhead)*

Comments: This passage of the *Bhagavad Gita* admits that meditation is superior to the studying of scriptures, austerity, and selfless service. In the end of it all, do you want to be in union with a god who lies and full of wrath, **anger and rage** as shown in the *Mahabharata* volume 2, book 9, Shalya Parva. The clarity of Krishna; **perjured** himself in the Mahabharata volume 2, book 7, Droan Parva 12 Arjuna's Dream; (a) he entered into **conflict** with Agni (fire god) and Arjuna (Indra's son), also in the Mahabharata story; (b) Krishna entered into **conflict** with Indra; and (c) Krishna entered into **conflict** with Shiva, also in the Mahabharata story. Therefore, for a vast majority of Hindu believer has no surety of the afterlife and are deign to the hundreds and possibly thousands of rebirths, and for some, they will devolve as per the doctrine. For a surety of eternal life, where mankind can be severed, the root of sin in their lives and conquer death and hell, not through the works of self-righteousness but by faith in Jesus Christ and His sacrifice on the cross for sin and His resurrection, and those who believe may have life eternal.

H. Yoga and Meditation

(i) Introduction

The end goal is the same and that is, to be as God or to be in union with God. The devotees are then chasing after self-righteousness by meditation and yogic meditation, but the result is the same. To be as god by willpower, strength, and determination of the soul, to deny all desires, wants, needs, feelings, etc. in order to attain immortality is to be as god with works of self-righteousness. There is no humility involved but strictly determination and willpower to deny and refuse all attachments and, therefore, victorious by the strength or power of your soul in pure stubbornness to conquer the flesh. Therefore, a devotee attains a passing grade by his own power, and he thinks he has arrived, but there is no evidence, and it is only temporary, and he will fall back to his old condition and has to fight the same battle over and over again.

Listed below are the evidence from the Hindu sacred text on the path of self-righteousness, the vanity of vanities. Even while the devotee is doing all these things, sin is still in him or her because the root of sin has not been severed. Sin is just suppressed. It speaks volume to the power of sin and its hold on humanity. The futility of doing, performing all the yogic meditation failed to sever your sins, must engender tremendous uncertainty of one's status in the afterdeath. If it took Indra 105 years as in Padma Purana to finish his training, what kind of chance do you think you have in attaining union in your lifetime with the Atman, Universal Spirit, Krishna, Brahma, or a foreign spiritual entity. To make the situation worse, Brahma and Shiva had no control of their lust and desires, and Shiva, Indra, Brahma, Krishna, and Vishnu are all deceivers.

(ii) Guide for Meditation and Kundalini Energy

(ii.a) Only in the meditative quietude and peace is it possible to be a Brahman, which is beyond any speech and its trappings. It is in that silence that the soul, mind, and the consciousness of the Absolute that a man finds the Brahman, the AUM, the eternal and unchanging. *(Mahabharata vol. 2, book 5 Udyoga Parva 7 A Blind King's Terror)*

Comments: Look what the Vishnu in Shiva Purana had to say about the AUM. Brahma comes from the letter *A*, signifying creation, Vishnu the letter *U*, signifying nurturement, and Shiva is from the letter *M*, signifying salvation. The A, U, and M are also metaphors for Brahma as semen and Vishnu for the vagina, as in the *Shiva*

Maha Purana 5.2 Shiva Samhita 5.2.9 Shabda-Brahma. Of course, M stands for Shivalinga, Shiva's penis. The OM sound is the mantra in Shiva.

(ii.b) It is traditional to meditate on Kusha grass and be seated on deerskin. Meditation must be single-minded and focused with total concentration. **The head, neck, and body must be in an absolute straight line so that the erect spinal column prevents drowsiness and allows the free flow of vital Kundalini energy.** *(Bhagavad Gita, chapter 6, The Practice of Meditation)*

Comments: The Kundalini energy is defined as the serpent power that is spiritual and evolutionary energy that is like a coiled force at the base of the spine that rises up through the body in the depths of meditation to awaken the higher center of consciousness.

This doctrine is very real in that the devotee will gain the power of the serpent power through meditation, and that is impossible to realize unless the serpent is in you. So it only makes sense that when the serpent enters into you, you will have the serpent's power. This is a confirmation of the previous text (the *Bhagavad Gita* chapter 8 "The Eternal Godhead" pp. 160–161 quoting the Chandogya Upanishad 8:6:5–6 as translated by Eknath Easwaran)) that tells you at the Atman or Universal Soul/Spirit, Krishna, Brahma, or Vishnu enter into you through the crown of the head, called sagittal aperture of Brahma and possesses you. It definitely is the Kundalini or serpent power because all the major deities are all personification of the serpent. You will be in unity with Krishna, Brahma, Shiva, and Vishnu, who are all deceivers, master of the maya, and some of them desired and lusted after another woman who is not their wife! And you want to be in union with any of them?

(ii.c) An untrained mind constantly wanders all over and is restless, trying to fulfil its desires. It must be brought back into focus and rest on the divine self. When in the depths of meditation, it stops wandering and find its fulfilment. The still mind touches the Brahman and enjoys the bliss. Krishna advises that it is very difficult to train the mind, but it is possible with regular practice and detachment. Krishna mentioned that it is possibly for a person to assume his spiritual quest for self-realization after a person dies and is into another family from where he had left off and will have a head start in the quest. *(Bhagavad Gita, chapter 6, The Practice of Meditation)*

Comments: It is speaking the truth in that it is difficult to break down the built-in wall of self-protection and self-preservation, but that doctrine is mixed with the things that are not true about self-realization and being born again and again. It is easier to swallow a lie if there is some truth laced with it. One cannot enjoy the bliss if void of feelings!

(ii.d) The mind is difficult to control, but with regular practice and detachment, it is possible to master it and attain the goal of self-realization; that means realizing the divine self in the person and in everything. *(Bhagavad Gita, chapter 6, The Practice of Meditation)*

Comments: Yes, it is difficult indeed, as all of us had been given a mechanism of protection in our consciousness, our mind, and our will. But the Atman, Krishna, Brahma, Universal Spirit, or foreign entity had found a way to destroy the self-will through discipline and determination in the practice of yogic meditation and the chanting of the mantram to take over the possession of the person!

(ii.e) When meditating, the mind must be completely still, and the concentration be fixed in between the eyebrows, the center of spiritual awareness. *(Bhagavad Gita, chapter 8, The Eternal Godhead)*

(iii) Purpose of Meditation

(iii.a) A man can **purify himself by washing away his desires** in the river because his atman or soul is sacred.

(iii.b) The **aim of meditation or tapasya is the inner peace** and quietude, not in speech only but also of the mind and senses. A person who achieved that is the Brahman and is the ultimate reality, that is, eternal and unchanging. AUM is the Brahman.

(iii.c) **The ultimate Brahman cannot be achieved in a lifetime but in several lifetimes.** The ultimate Brahman cannot be understood nor defined, and it cannot be found in the akasa or the very essence of all things, in the Devas nor in the Vedas, but it is present in all things. Even the cosmic destroyer, Lord Shiva, is destroyed by it after the dissolution. *(Mahabharata vol. 2 book 5, Udyoga Parva, 7. A Blind King's Terror)*

Comments: (a) Sin, impurity of thoughts and feelings, and evil acts are not physical material things that can be washed away in the river. (b) Quietude and inner peace is not the true purpose of meditation, as the purpose is to achieve union with the divine self by becoming selfless and allowing the foreign spirit to enter the devotee, as in sections E (v) and H (vi). (c) To achieve the ultimate Brahman may take a hundred lifetime. However, you may be caught in the Samsara cycle as if it is at the end of the Kalpa or age when the whole creation will be destroyed and creation will restart. Where then will you be? You may come back as a Neanderthal man, and if you devolve you may come back as a dinosaur. Does it sound reasonable or intelligent to you? You will never know if you had earned sufficient merits to overcome your demerits because you do not know what the rules of the game are, as it had never been published. It seemed to me that Krishna had good days and bad days, so your salvation is in jeopardy, and it depends on the whims of Krishna.

(iv) Reciting the Vedas will not save

Reciting the Vedas does not save a deceitful man. *(Mahabharata vol. 2 book 5, Udyoga Parva, 7 A Blind King's Terror)*

Comment: Save a deceitful man from what? Going through the Samsara cycle, but then as in (ii) so what if it took 100 or 101 lifetime, what difference does that make? This doctrine is contrary, as Krishna is a deceitful god, as he is the lord of the maya (deceit or illusion), and he perjured himself. And if Krishna, a deceitful man, is immortal and an avatar of Vishnu, you cannot do any worse! But then so are Vishnu, Indra, Brahma, and Shiva, etc.

(v) A Bondage from Free Will?

The path of perfect renunciation is difficult to attain without performing action, but nevertheless, it leads to freedom of bondage of free will. The wiser follows the path of selfless service after they had completely purified themselves and conquered their senses and self-will. *(Bhagavad Gita, chapter 5, Renounce and Rejoice)*

Comments: Again, this doctrine is false as shown in section E (v), in that it destroys the self-will and not as the passage tries to tell you as "freedom from the bondage of free will." **Free will is NOT a bondage** but RIGHT that allows mankind to choose for him or herself. If destroying the self-will is to be free of bondage, then that statement is true. If you lost your free will, who then are you? A person who lost his free will meant that someone else is in control of that free will, and that someone else is in control of you, thus possession by a foreign entity or spirit. In many countries, its citizens had lost their rights to free will when living under an autocratic ruler, and in the same vein in the spiritual realm, the devotee lost his or her free will to a spiritual entity. In many countries, for a person to exercise his or her free will means being disowned by relatives and be separated from friends and peers. The quest for truth requires courage and a relentless pursuit, which is sometimes very costly, but the noble quest is worth more than its weight of gold.

(vi) Entrance of Krishna into a Person or Possession

When a person enters into deep meditation, called Samadhi, the breathing is steady and is slowed down, and all senses are cut off. The mind quiets down, and all emotions and anger fade, and all senses and emotion disappear. **Now the spirit (Krishna) is free to flow, and a person enters into a state called Samadhi,** and the long duration in the state of Samadhi can only be achieved after many years of dedication. Once it is established, a person lives in permanent spiritual freedom. *(Bhagavad Gita, chapter 5, Renounce and Rejoice)*

Comments: When dedicating yourself to daily meditation to deny yourself of everything, including the taking care or the neglect of your family is selfishness to the extreme. The shunning of your responsibilities and letting others support your family, or at worse make your children beg in the streets or be sold. This deep meditation is nothing but the technique to suppress all your wants, desires, needs, anger, lusts for the sake of being at one with God. All that is for the purpose of destroying the self-will that the foreign entity or spirit is invited to enter into you so that you can be at one with the foreign entity. It is superdangerous because you have no control of the foreign spirit at all. That is why I call it possession. When it talks about spiritual freedom, it meant that the foreign spirit, entity, or even a demon(s) had full control to do whatever it so desires. **So to call it spiritual freedom is a lie when in reality it is spiritual bondage**. If Krishna is already in everything, as in section A (iv), why is there a need to enter into another person or possess another body? When Krishna enters into you, then he is in possession of you.

(vii) A Yogi

A yogi is a person who does meditation and is not about posture or exercise. To discover self-realization is like climbing a mountain or shana and get more difficult as you approach the summit. Willpower, self-help, and intense effort is absolutely necessary. For those who reached the summit will find the truest friend in the self (Krishna or the Atman). Only those who are self-disciplined and conquered himself live in peace. He will not have malice nor look upon anyone as a foe and he has achieved a perfect mind and attitude or sambuddhi. The yogi had achieved in him all levels of consciousness and feels everyone's joy and sorrow as if it is their own. They see the self in all beings. *(Bhagavad Gita, chapter 6, The Practice of Meditation)*

Comments: Do you ever see a yogi in meditation lying in bed, sitting on a chair by the kitchen table, or standing by a tree? Never. Please read (ii.b) below about the posture. It must start in a serpentine posture and be aware of the kundalini or serpentine power. It is a contradiction because a yogi is void of feelings and desires and therefore cannot feel anyone's joy or sorrow.

(viii) The Yogi State of Mind

(viii.a) The will is a friend for those who have conquered themselves but an enemy for those who failed to find the self within. For those who had conquered themselves, they are in touch with the supreme reality and live in peace as there is no cold or hot, pleasure or pain, and praise or blame and had arrived at the apex of human consciousness. There is no difference between dirt, stone or gold, friends, family or enemies. **Good and evil are alike.** *(Bhagavad Gita, chapter 6, The Practice of Meditation)*

Comments: In Christianity, to say that good and evil are alike is also saying that God and Satan is the same entity! But in the *Bhagavad Gita.* that is the doctrine that's preached and accepted.

It is always easier to sell a lie by attaching the lie with some truths, and this is one of the many examples: "the good and evil are alike." So why are men so gullible? It is a deception that had been used over and over again because it works. The desire to be as God and immortality blinds the person. If evil is like good, then there is no need to jail those who did wrong. If evil is really as it is good, then they should actually celebrate every time someone commits evil. If a person cannot see the difference in the duality of life, then he is like a dead person with no conscience or feelings at all, but then, that is the whole object of complete renunciation and being complete free of attachments.

This, the constant effort of meditation, breaks down the wall of what the text called "self-will" that allows possession of the person to take place. So if you cannot see that this doctrine from the *Bhagavad Gita* is a lie, then there is a real problem, as you had just been deceived! But if it is telling the truth, then Brahma, Vishnu, Rama, Krishna, Shiva are both good and evil. So how can anyone be serious about the Bhagavad Gita, which preaches both some truths and mostly lies, as that is in line with the personality that comes from the deceiver or serpent? It is very consistent behavior, and you should not be surprised at all. One false doctrine or lie spoils the whole lot because if only just one lie is discovered, then there will be a whole bunch. Even a little bit of yeast will leaven the whole loaf. It can no longer be trusted: the doctrine, God, and preacher!

(viii.b) With constant effort detaching from the mind and desire, the person is absorbed into the divine self, and when it is mastered, the self will reveal itself, and the devotee will know the joy and peace that is beyond the senses. *(Bhagavad Gita, chapter 6, The Practice of Meditation)*

Comments: What it meant is that once the self-will is destroyed, the foreign or so-called divine spirit will take over. This is the possession of the spirit or foreign entity in a body. This is precisely the way we are created—with a will, a mind, and conscience—so that evil spirits or demons cannot take possession of the body. And this doctrine is essentially getting a person to lower all his protection so that a foreign spirit or demon can possess the body. In the Christian Bible, many times Jesus cast out demons from the possessed people. There are many people who are possessed by demons, foreign entities or spirits without being aware of them, and this is true in this twenty-first century.

(ix.a) Be One with the Divine or God

When the meditation is mastered, the two consciousness (yours and the divine self) are unified, and they see everything with the same eye. *(Bhagavad Gita, chapter 6, The Practice of Meditation)*

Comments: It definitely is not unified when one's own is destroyed! How is it a union when the self-will is destroyed? It is very much one-sided as the person is no longer in control of himself! To call it union is a falsehood as it is more than the self (Krishna or the Atman) will dominate the person when his will is destroyed. Your own will is not strong enough to dominate that of a foreign entity or spirit.

(ix.b) A person is purified and attains self-realization after many lifetimes of purification of all selfish desires. Meditation is superior to asceticism or the path of knowledge, and it is also superior to selfless service. Those who had mastered meditation are firmly established in me and absorbed into me and worships me with perfect faith. *(Bhagavad Gita, chapter 6, The Practice of Meditation)*

Comments: To reject or renounce his own parents, wife, and children to chase after self-realization for himself is itself a selfish act and, therefore, contrary to its own doctrine! To be at one or union with a master of the maya or deception cannot but make you a deceiver and a liar also!

(x) Failure to be with the Divine or as One with God

(x.a) The path of wisdom is regarded as possibly too steep for all humans. *(Bhagavad Gita, chapter 12, The way of Love)*

Comments: It is impossible to be fully realized, free of attachments, and renounced everything and to have any feeling of love for anything at all. They are diametrically opposite to each other. Yes, it is too steep and therefore unreachable for 99.9 percent of the Indian Hindu population. So what is Brahma, Vishnu, or Shiva's intent when creating humans when only the elite or very, very few can attain union with the divine spirit and be as god? It is their intent that 99.9 percent of their creature spend most of their life in misery and suffering because they had set the criteria for attaining immortality too high or unreachable for 99.9 percent of the population? Is that what you call divine love?

(x.b) When a person fails in realizing the divine self, the person is not destroyed when he dies **because he is a good person,** but they go to other realms where the righteous live. They live there for countless years and then reborn into a family where meditation is practiced, and to born into such a family is rare. The wisdom that they had acquired in their previous lives are stirred up again, and they will strive harder for self-realization. *(Bhagavad Gita, chapter 6, The Practice of Meditation)*

Comments: Who and what defines a good person? All had sinned and is not morally perfect and therefore had demerits, and how is he to know if had had more merits than demerits? This doctrine of self-realization requires someone who is morally perfect in order to ascend or be illuminated and acquire the Atman or divine spirit. Who is morally perfect or be able to reach perfection? Otherwise, you will spend hundreds or even thousands of years in deaths and rebirths, and you may even be cut off midway because at the end of the age or kalpa, everything is destroyed and then regenerated. Again, what is taught here is a lie because it is deign for man to live

233

once then to die and face eternal judgment, as there is no continual rebirths. There is no proof that wisdom is accumulated from previous lives because mankind continually fights wars that they start and never seemed to have learned from history, even when it is written and published and taught in schools.

(x.c) If regular attempts at meditation fail, one should work tirelessly without desire for the results of his labor, as real peace comes from renunciation. Self-surrender is the last resort, but it does bring immediate peace. *(Bhagavad Gita, chapter 12, The way of Love)*

Comments: It is impossible to be fully realized, free of attachments, and renounced everything to feel peace, as the person will have no feeling at all. If good and evil are alike, then war and peace is the same, as you have no feeling toward either. You might as well be a rock or a log and therefore achieve self-realization, illumination and be at one with the divine spirit. When you cannot stop to smell the flowers, appreciate a beautiful sunset, be thankful for kind deeds, and empathize with the less fortunate or help them, then you might as well be log or a rock because to have those feelings is not to have fully renounced them.

(xi) Successful Yogis

(xi.a) The ones who are most established in yoga are those who set their hearts and worship me with steadfast faith and devotion. Similarly, those that seek the divine reality that has no name nor form and contemplating on the Unmanifested Krishna that is outside the reach of their thoughts and feelings, while striving for the good of all, will eventually be united with Krishna. *(Bhagavad Gita, chapter 12, The Way of Love)*

Comments: If a person is fully realized, then he or she is successful in renouncing all wants, needs, desires, feelings, and therefore free of attachments. Then how can a person then worship, as a log or a rock cannot worship Krishna? To want to worship involves the will and desire and a love, and in this case, there is none of those attributes, and therefore, it is impossible to worship.

(xii) An Alternative to an Unsuccessful Yogi

Difficult is the way of meditation, but if a person has me as his supreme goal and work at renouncing his self to me and meditate on me single-mindedly, I will rescue him from the death and birth cycle because his consciousness had entered into Krishna. If a person still cannot still his mind through the regular practice of meditation through the lack of self-discipline or will, he can still find complete fulfillment through selfless service. *(Bhagavad Gita, Chapter 12, The Way of Love)*

Comments: You cannot provide "selfless service" when you interact with humans because the interaction will activate all your five senses. Can you stand by a starving and crying baby and behave like a log or rock because that is what this doctrine of self-realization is asking you to? If that is what it takes for immortality, then that is selfish and not worth its weight in gold! When a person is fully possessed by a foreign spirit or demon, then he or she behaves exactly like a log or rock, as he or she had absolutely lost control of himself or herself. And is this the way of love?

(xiii) Krishna Loves Only the Successful Ones

(xiii.a) Knowledge is better than mechanical practice, but meditation is better than knowledge. However, better still is the surrender of attachment to results because one attains immediate peace. The ones that I, Krishna, love are those you live beyond the dualities of life, like pleasure and pain, and beyond the I and mine, in self-control, focused in faith and had given me all their heart and their mind to me. *(Bhagavad Gita, chapter 12, The Way of Love)*

Comments: Krishna cannot love because he is fully realized, free of attachments, and had renounced everything and therefore cannot have any feelings and can never love. The fact that Krishna married to Rukmini, Satyabhama, Kalindi, Mitrvinda, Sattya, and Bhadra (and not mentioning the 16,000 women prisoners he saved, released, and married to) should tell you that he had feelings, desires, and lots of sex. So all this talk about Krishna is fully self-realized, free of attachment, and had successfully renounced all desires and lust is just a lie. So if Krishna is a liar, how then can you possibly believe anything he says? The same applies for Vishnu, Shiva, Brahma, and Indra, etc.

(xiii.b) The one who is dear to Krishna are those that had conquered the dualities of life and are unmoved by anything that life dishes out. They are pure, detached, efficient, impartial, never anxious, and selfless and are Krishna's devotees. *(Bhagavad Gita, chapter 12, The Way of Love)*

Comments: Krishna is not SELFLESS but SELFISH because he had married 16,108 women and did not give them away to someone else. It is like hoarding, and with that many women, he deprived many of not having children at all, unless you tell me that he had serviced them all!

(xiii.c) The ones who are dear to Krishna are those who are not affected by praise or blame, success or failure, honor or dishonor, and is ever quiet and in harmony and is strong in faith. *(Bhagavad Gita, chapter 12, The Way of Love)*

Comments: Krishna already admitted or confessed that he is the lord of deception, as in the *Bhagavad Gita, chapter 7, Wisdom & Realization*, so why would anyone believe in any of his claims. And in *Bhagavad Gita, chapter 10, Divine Splendor,* Krishna is described as a demon, and that makes it even worse.

I. Self-Realization and Yoga Mantram

(i) Krishna defines the oldest Hindu or holy and spiritual sound of OM (or AUM), TAT and SAT, which is the sacred syllable that is Brahma. Om is the sound that is heard when in deep meditation. *Tat* is the supreme reality that is beyond thought or spoken words, and *sat* means that which is. The mantram of om, tat, sat confirms that good really exists, and the opposite is Asat, which means that evil is transient and therefore cannot not be impermanent and not real. Any action without faith or shraddha is Asat and not real. *(Bhagavad Gita, chapter 17, The Power of Faith)*

Comments: Om, tat, and sat was not inexistent during the Vedic times. It is a means to dull the mind and break down or destroy the self-will, as in section C (iv).

(ii) Repeated Priestly Chants

The priests would repeatedly chant the mantram of om, tat, and sat when performing sacrifices and reciting the scriptures or offering gifts. Those who seek liberation without rewards would add the word tat and sat, used to describe goodness, like a worthy deed. And to practice without faith is ASAT. *(Bhagavad Gita, chapter 17, The Power of Faith)*

Comments: Same as in Section C (iv)

(iii) Repeated Chants in the Vedas

The Gayatri mantra consisted of twenty-four letters, and each one is the name of a specific deity. For example first is Agni, second is Vayu, third is Surya, ninth is Indra, twelfth is Mitra, twentieth is Prajapati, twenty-second is Rudra, twenty-third is Brahma, and the last is Vishnu. The person who chants this Gayatri mantra one hundred times will be free from their sins, obtains salvation, and is bestowed virtues similar to that received from studying the four Vedas. *(Padma Purana 2.1.12 An Ideal Brahmin and the Significance of the Gayatri Mantra)*

Comments: The Gayatri mantra is passe and no longer practice or one can say that it is no longer relevant. Agni, Surya, Indra, Mitra, etc. are no longer worshipped and, therefore, became irrelevant. And to think that a mighty god can become irrelevant just blows one's mind. If they are of no use today, then they are of no use yesterday. And if the Vedas had been documenting and promoting them, then it is all in vain because it is all a lie. And if the origin is a lie, what then becomes of what it had become? A lie cannot, because of progress, become truth. Only lies can come from lies. If the Vedas is teaching the truth about Mitra, Surya, Agni, Nasatyas, (all vedic deities), then they should be worshipped today! The same Vedas record many gods, like Varuna, Mitra, Asvins, Agni, etc., that had become irrelevant today. And as you can already see in India today, the popularity of Shiva, Brahma, Indra, Krishna, and Vishnu had faded in their popularity and are being replaced by the many other gods. It sounds like a popularity and functionality contest, and the past gods and deities had become relevant, and if relevant now, they must also be relevant in the past.

(iv) Significance of A U M

Shiva appeared as a sage to Vishnu and Brahma to explain the AUM and the mantra OM. Brahma comes from the letter *A*, signifying creation, Vishnu the letter *U*, signifying nurturement, and Shiva is from the letter *M*, signifying salvation. The A, U, and M are also metaphors for Brahma as semen and Vishnu for the vagina. Of course, M stands for Shivalinga, the penis. The OM sound is the mantra of Shiva. *(Shiva Maha Purana 5.2 Shiva Samhita 5.2.9 Shabda-Brahma)*

Comments: **Why** would anyone be reciting those sounds that represent the sexual organs and semen of so-called gods? It is in reality perverse.

Glossary: The Source of Biblical Quotations

Acts and Luke:

Luke (~AD 30–74) was a native of Antioch in Syria, a physician at the time of Jesus, and a follower of Jesus. He authored the Gospel of Luke and the Acts. The Acts was a record and description of the events and what the apostles did after the death and resurrection of Jesus.

Colossians:

This epistle was written by the apostle Paul to the church in Colossae in Asia Minor (present-day Turkey), probably sometime before AD 80.

1 Corinthians and 2 Corinthians

The letters were written to the Christians living in the city of Corinth in Greece by the apostle Paul, who was a Jewish Pharisee from Tarsus in Eastern Turkey. He was born around 4 BC and died around AD 64–66 in Rome. Paul persecuted Christians in Jerusalem until he had a spiritual experience of a vision from Jesus, who was resurrected from the dead. He became blind, was healed, and became a Christian and preached the Gospel of Jesus until his death in Rome.

Ecclesiastes:

Some claimed this is another book of wisdom authored by King Solomon around the year 937 BC.

Ephesians:

This is another epistle by the apostle Paul to the church in Ephesus, present-day Turkey, probably around the year AD 62, while he was a prisoner in Rome.

Exodus:

The family (seventy) of Jacob fled the famine in the land and lived in Egypt (1800 BC) through Jacob's son, Joseph, who was a high official of the Pharaoh in Egypt. But they suffered as slaves under a new Pharaoh for four hundred years. Moses was chosen by God at the age of eighty to lead the people out of slavery and suffering and into the promised land of Canaan. The exodus started around 1446 BC, and the people wandered in the desert for forty years because of sin. During the time of wandering in the desert, God gave the Ten Commandments, ordinances, and statutes, as well as instructions of sacrifices for sins and instructions for the construction of the tabernacle to the people through Moses. Moses, because of disobedience, did not enter into the promised land of Canaan, but it was Joshua who led them into the promised land.

Galatians:

The epistle to the Galatians is a letter written by the Apostle Paul to the Christian communities living in Galatia, Turkey. The original was written around AD 50, in papyrus, and only fragments were found and preserved.

Genesis:

This is the first book of five written by Moses of the Bible. Moses (~1525 BC–1645 BC), a descendant of Abraham, was born to a family of Hebrew people who were slaves in Egypt. He was adopted by the daughter of the Pharaoh of Egypt, killed an Egyptian, and fled into the desert. God called him to free the Hebrews.

Hebrews:

The author of the book entitled *Hebrews* is unknown by biblical scholars but deduced that it was written around AD 64, by a Hellenic

Jewish Christian during the period of strong Christian persecution. It was written to exhort Christians to persevere in the face of death and imprisonment. The writing is about the person of Jesus Christ as a mediator between God and humanity.

Isaiah (Old Testament prophet):
Isaiah is one of the greatest prophets of the Bible, and his ministry is around 740 BC to 698 BC. The Book of Isaiah had been quoted some ten times in the New Testament of the Bible with regard to the prophecies of the suffering of the Messiah, Jesus of Nazareth, and how He would die to save mankind from their sins and that He is to be the Light of the World to both Jews and Gentiles (non-Jews).

James (Half-brother of Jesus):
There were two James in the New Testament of the Bible. One is James, the brother of John, both of whom were sons of Zebedee. The other James is the earthly brother of Jesus. Jesus, the Son of God, was the son of Mary, who was impregnated by the Holy Spirit, and therefore did not have an earth father. James was the son of Mary and a carpenter by the name of Joseph; therefore, James was the half-brother of Jesus, who grew up with Jesus. James was an elder in the church in Jerusalem in around AD 62. James was thrown from the roof of the temple, then beaten and clubbed to death.

Jeremiah (Old Testament prophet):
Jeremiah is a prophet of the Old Testament of the Bible in around the year 626 BC. He was called by God to turn the people toward repentance for idol worship and idolatrous practices, like the neighbouring nations of Israel. The people at that time had rejected the laws, ordinances, and statutes given by God through Moses. Jeremiah warned them of the dire consequences of their actions.

John (an apostle of Jesus):
The teaching and inspired gospel was written by John, the son of Zebedee (AD 30–90), was an apostle and follower of Jesus during the three years of Jesus's ministry on earth, and a witness to all Jesus

had said and done. John also wrote three other epistles (1, 2, and 3 John), and the book of Revelations.

Leviticus:

Leviticus is the third book of the Old Testament of the Bible written by Moses (~1525–1645 BC), and the writing contains the law, ordinances, and statutes of God for the people so they can live a life that will be blessed by Him and what to do in order for God to forgive their sins.

Malachi (Old Testament prophet):

The prophet Malachi wrote his book to the Jews who had returned from their exile in Persia, modern-day Iran, to remind them of God's punishment and to return to God in how they conduct their religious, social, and daily lives. Malachi's ministry was just before 445 BC.

Mark:

The Gospel of Mark was written by John Mark around AD 70 and is thought to be the first gospel written. He did not appear on the scene until after the resurrection of Jesus. John Mark accompanied the apostle Paul and Barnabas on their first missionary journey to Cyprus.

Matthew (An apostle of Jesus):

Matthew was one of the twelve disciples and an apostle of Jesus. Matthew was also a witness to the resurrection and ascension of Jesus. He was a tax collector and, therefore, despised by the Jews. Matthew was speared to death for preaching the gospel in the city of Nadabah (Ethiopia) in AD 60.

Micah (Old Testament prophet):

Micah was an Old Testament prophet around 737 to 696 BC, and he authored the Book of Micah. He warned and prophesied during the reign of kings Jotham, Ahaz, and Hezekiah regarding idolatry and the destruction of Jerusalem. Micah also prophesied where the coming Messiah, Jesus, would be born.

Numbers (~1445 BC):
This is one of the five books written by Moses, and it begins in Mount Sinai where the Israelites, through Moses, received the laws and covenants from God. It is called the *Book of Numbers* because the people were numbered, and preparations were made for the continuance of their journey to the promised land of Canaan.

Peter (An apostle of Jesus):
The two books, 1 and 2 Peter, were written by the apostle Simon Peter for the believers living outside Israel, and most likely the ones living in the Roman Provinces in Asia Minor, present-day Turkey, sometime around AD 60.

Philippians:
This was an epistle written by the apostle Paul to the believers in Philippi of Greece, which he and Timothy had visited in their second missionary journey in around AD 49–51.

Psalms:
The Psalms is a collection of inspired writings, most of which (73 of 150) were by King David (~1035–961 BC) who was born in Bethlehem and was the second king of Israel. When he was just a youngster, he killed the giant of a man, Goliath of the Philistines, who stood some 2.97 meters tall, with a stone from a slingshot. David, the son of Jesse, was chosen by God and anointed by the prophet Samuel to be king of Israel, and he walked with God all the days of his life.

Revelations:
Revelations is a book of prophecies by the Apostle John, the son of Zebedee, a disciple of Jesus, around AD 90 when he was imprisoned and exiled on the island of Patmos. It is a book of wars and natural and unnatural disasters here on earth, as well as in the heavens, that affect all mankind and how Jesus will come to judge all, including Satan and his fallen angels, and to present a new hope for those who are saved in Him.

Romans:

The apostle Paul wrote the epistle or letter (~AD 30–55) to the Romans, and it is one of the most profound and important in Christian doctrine. It explained how mankind is under bondage or slavery to *sin* under the law, and how the law of the spirit of life through Jesus Christ sets us free. Not only do we receive eternal life when we accept Jesus, the Son of God, who was crucified on the cross and then resurrected from the dead, but that the Spirit of God sets us free from bondage to sin and the flesh.

1 Thessalonians and 2 Thessalonians

The first letter to the church in Thessalonica was written by the apostle Paul probably around AD 52 when he was in Corinth, Greece. The second letter was probably written around AD 52–54.

Zechariah

The Jewish prophet Zechariah (ministry in ~520–480 BC) lived during the time of Darius the Great of Persia after the fall of Jerusalem and after the Jewish exile years in Babylon. Zechariah's burden was for the Jewish people to repent and return to God and declare his Messianic prophecy concerning Jesus.

Life-Changing Action
(for all Buddhists and any
interested parties)

A. If you are unable to suppress all your terrible desires, wants, lusts, and cravings;

B. if you do not want to be stuck for years in the Samsara cycle;

C. if no one can provide you with an answer to where and what Nirvana is; and

D. if you find that you are unable to save yourself.

Then come to the Lord Jesus Christ, the son of God, who was crucified for your sin, which are many, and was resurrected from the dead that you may have life eternal, which is without pain or tears, full of everlasting joy, praise, and worship, and inherit the Kingdom of God. This can and will happen immediately, and you do not have to wait. You will be set free from self-condemnation and from the law of sin and death.

Here are the promises of God, and He does not and cannot lie:

(i) John 3:3–7; 16 says,

Jesus answered and said to him, "Truly, truly, I say to you, unless one is born again he cannot see the kingdom of God." Nicodemus said to Him, "How can a man be born when he is old? He cannot enter a second time into

245

his mother's womb and be born, can he?" Jesus answered, "Truly, truly, I say to you, unless one is born of water and the Spirit he cannot enter into the kingdom of God. That which is born of the flesh is flesh, and that which is born of the Spirit is spirit. Do not be amazed that I said to you, 'You must be born again.'"

For God so loved the world, that He gave His only begotten Son, that whoever believes in Him shall not perish, but have eternal life.

(ii) Revelation 21:3–4 says, "And I heard a loud voice from the throne, saying, 'Behold, the tabernacle of God is among men, and He will dwell among them, and they shall be His people, and God Himself will be among them, and He will wipe away every tear from their eyes; and there will no longer be any death; there will no longer be any mourning, or crying, or pain; the first things have passed away.'"

(iii) Galatians 5:22–25 says, "But the fruit of the Spirit is love, joy, peace, patience, kindness, goodness, faithfulness, gentleness, self-control; against such things there is no law. Now those who belong to Christ Jesus have crucified the flesh with its passions and desires. If we live by the Spirit, let us also walk by the Spirit."

(iv) Romans 8:1–2; 10–14 says,

Therefore there is now no condemnation for those who are in Christ Jesus. For the law of the Spirit of life in Christ Jesus has set you free from the law of sin and of death. If Christ is in you, though the body is dead because of sin, yet the spirit is alive because of righteousness.

But if the Spirit of Him who raised Jesus from the dead dwells in you, He who raised Christ Jesus from the dead will also give life to your mortal bodies through His Spirit who dwells in you.

So then, brethren, we are under obligation, not to the flesh, to live according to the flesh—for if you are living according to the flesh, you must die; but if by the Spirit you are putting to death the deeds of the body, you will live.

(v) Romans 10:8–10 says, "But what does it say? *'The word is near you,* in your mouth and in your heart'—that is, the word of faith which we are preaching, that if you confess with your mouth Jesus as Lord, and believe in your heart that God raised Him from the dead, you will be saved; for with the heart a person believes, resulting in righteousness, and with the mouth he confesses, resulting in salvation."

(vi) First John 1:9–10 says, "If we confess our sins, He is faithful and righteous to forgive us our sins and to cleanse us from all unrighteousness. If we say that we have not sinned, we make Him a liar and His word is not in us."

(vii) Romans 8:10–11 says, "If Christ is in you, though the body is dead because of sin, yet the spirit is alive because of righteousness. But if the Spirit of Him who raised Jesus from the dead dwells in you, He who raised Christ Jesus from the dead will also give life to your mortal bodies through His Spirit who dwells in you."

So if you are ready to be a follower of Jesus Christ and receive the promises of God, then here are two simple steps to take:

1. Confess your sins, which are many, and ask God for forgiveness. (For example, speak or say out loud, "God, please forgive me for my sins, which are many.")
2. Accept the sacrifice that God had made for sins. (For example, speak or say out loud, "I accept Jesus Christ, your begotten Son and my Saviour, who was crucified on the

cross for my sins and was resurrected that I may have life everlasting.")

If you had done steps 1 and 2, you are immediately brought into the kingdom of God and receive eternal life. That means you are saved forever from eternal damnation and hell, and the Spirit of God comes into you and lives in you (that means the Spirit of God is born in you, i.e., born again, and that is why you can now call God your heavenly Father). Now you have become a follower of Jesus Christ. To help you understand what you had done and to begin your walk as a follower of Jesus Christ, try and find an evangelical Christian church in your community that can teach you the fundamentals of your faith.

I accept Jesus Christ as Saviour on this ___ day of ____ (month), 20____.

Signed (your name) _____

About the Author

Norman Law graduated from the University of Alberta, Canada, in 1970, and retired as an engineering project manager after working thirty-eight of his forty-four years in the oil and gas industry in Canada.

Norman published his first book in 2016, *Qur'an Bible Study Commentary*, which compared the complete Qur'an (114 Surahs) with the doctrines in the Christian Bible. He then published his second book, *Buddha and the Man on the Cross*, in 2018. In his six years of research into the ancient Vedic sacred Hindu texts for his third book *Hinduism and the Man on the Cross*, he discovered the many origins of the major Buddhist doctrines and practices, and how they were modified and changed a thousand years later, so he decided to include his findings in the second edition of the book.

In his early years, Norman went to school and grew up with folks from different faiths, like Roman Catholicism, Hinduism, Islam, and Buddhism. His search for "meaning of life" started in 1974. He met and received the Lord Jesus as his Saviour on November 1, 1976.

Norman was married for twenty-four years and widowed in 2005, has two adult children, and remarried Miss A. Akbari in 2018.

In February 2018, Norman almost died three times in three days from various incidents: a flood, a six-foot-long and four inches thick tree branch fell from a forest canopy, and a traffic incident.

Norman suffered a kidney failure on October 31, 2018, when his heart stopped twice and was resuscitated back to life in the emergency ward in the hospital and then again in the ICU. All glory and praise be to God, my Saviour for his mercy, grace, and blessings.